Human Needs
and
Intellectual Disabilities:

Ap ... *ning,*
L ... *tion*

Advance Praise for

Human Needs and Intellectual Disabilities:

Applications for Person Centered Planning, Dual Diagnosis, and Crisis Intervention

[Professor Steven Reiss's] capacity to integrate and make sense of literature from behavioral science, western philosophy and developmental disabilities has never been more instructive, and more entertaining, than in his new book: *Human Needs and Intellectual Disabilities: Applications for Person Centered Planning, Dual Diagnosis and Crisis Intervention....* Steven Reiss' *Human Needs and Intellectual Disabilities* is yet another of his many sterling contributions to the literature on identifying the needs of people with intellectual disabilities so that the proper steps can be taken to address those needs.

David Braddock, Ph.D.,
The Coleman-Turner Chair and Professor in Psychiatry,
University of Colorado Denver School of Medicine

Dr. Reiss has added a must-have resource for anyone working with persons with intellectual disabilities, especially those working with persons with co-morbid mental illness. Dr. Reiss adds a valuable new dimension, that of motivation, to the evaluation of behavior problems in persons with ID that can greatly enhance our approach to this most challenging population.

Earl L. Loschen, M.D.
Co-editor *DM-ID*

This book is an invaluable resource for those who work with individuals with intellectual disabilities. Dr. Reiss' innovative, scientifically-based approaches bring a new level of understanding of how to use each person's unique, individual needs to help them develop more happy, meaningful lives.

David Laman, Ph.D.
Founder and Director
Developmental Enhancement, PLC

This fascinating book by Dr. Reiss brings out some new concepts in assessing an individual with intellectual disability's on-going needs, outlining methods for assessing not only a person's immediate needs but his/her desires for a meaningful life. His methods seem quite practical and also are very respectful of the individual—he considers each one as a person of worth.

Ann R. Poindexter, M.D.
Consultant/Author

This book is dedicated to the graduate and postdoctoral students I mentored at the University of Illinois at Chicago (1972-1991) and at the Ohio State University (1992-2007).

James Wiltz, Ph.D.	needs, intellectual disabilities, dual diagnosis
Marc J. Tasse, Ph.D.	dual diagnosis
Susan Havercamp, Ph.D.	needs, intellectual disabilities, dual diagnosis
David M. Gursky, Ph.D.	psychology of fear
Denise Valenti-Hein, Ph.D.	skills training, intellectual disabilities
David Laman, Ph.D.	dual diagnosis (especially affective disorder)
Roberta Maller, Ph.D.	anxiety sensitivity
Marie Davidson, Ph.D.	adult children
Marie Nucci, Ph.D.	coping skills and intellectual disabilities
Grant Levitan, Ph.D.	diagnostic overshadowing
Wendy Epstein, Ph.D.	anxiety sensitivity
Richard J. McNally, Ph.D.	anxiety sensitivity
Diane Signatur, M.A.	open classrooms
Nestor Dyhdalo, Ph.D.	open classrooms
Mary Ellen Milos, Ph.D.	children's play
James Napolitan, Ph.D.	self-injurious behavior

Aristotle's Doctrine of the Mean *Nichomachean Ethics* (Book II)

I call a mean in relation to us that which is neither
excessive nor deficient,
and this is not one and the same for all.

Preface

Certain needs, such as food, companionship, safety, and independence, are common to the human species and, thus, are called *human needs*. At the dawn of scientific psychology William James (1918/1890) and William McDougall (2003/1908) -- and later William Murray (1938) and Abraham Maslow (1954) – provided lists of human needs. Unfortunately, the early psychologists did not provide scientifically valid lists, relied too much on controversial assessment methods called "projective techniques," and, moreover, did a poor job of applying human needs to practical issues.

For more than a decade my colleagues and I have been working to revive interest in theories of human needs. During that time, we empirically derived 16 such needs and presented scientific evidence of their reliability and validity. Everybody embraces all 16 needs, although we prioritize them differently. These priorities are what make us individuals.

We have successfully applied human needs to a number of practical activities including executive job coaching, marriage counseling, and school psychology. In sports psychology, Peter Boltersdorf and Frank Mantek used the 16 human needs in coaching Germany's Matthias Steiner, who won the gold medal for weightlifting at the 2008 Beijing Olympics. Boltersdorf also assisted coaches of the world champion 2007 German national handball team.

In this book, 12 human needs relevant to adolescents and adults with intellectual disabilities (ID) are discussed. Readers will see how an analysis of an individual's needs could be used for person-centered planning, assessment of dual diagnosis, and minimizing violence and challenging behavior for people who have a dual diagnosis. Specifically, readers will learn how needs analysis can replace generic thinking ("person with ID") with thinking about an individual's qualities and uniqueness (e.g., "he is friendly," "she is organized"). Because people are happy when their needs are met, but unhappy when their needs are frustrated, analysis of a person's needs can lead to numerous practical ideas for enhancing happiness and quality of life. Particularly for a person with a dual diagnosis (both intellectual disorder and mental illness), analysis of human needs can show how to anticipate what might frustrate the individual and, thus, possibly trigger episodes of challenging behavior. By more completely addressing each individual's needs, some episodes of challenging behavior might be avoided.

Organization of Book

The first four chapters of this book define 12 human needs and apply them to person-centered planning, focusing on the assessment of an individual's preferred lifestyle. The discussion encompasses psychological research on human needs as well as scholarly philosophical writings on such complex phenomena as happiness, purpose, motive, quality of life, and choice.

The next five chapters apply the 12 human needs to dual diagnosis and challenging behavior. These chapters provide an authoritative summary of what is known about the co-occurrence of psychiatric disorders and intellectual disabilities. Also included is a chapter on abnormal motivation, which has too often been a neglected topic in psychiatric literature.

The final chapter applies human needs to middle and high school students with poor grades. In this chapter the construct of achievement motivation is broken down into six components, providing a novel analysis of why some students struggle with poor grades.

Table of Contents

Chapter 1

Value-Based Happiness

Those only are happy…[who] have their minds fixed on
some object other than their own happiness
– J. S. Mill

I n the journal article "Introduction: The happiness in all our lives," Crocker (2000) encouraged a positive psychology approach to intellectual disabilities. He urged us to pay less attention to people's deficiencies and greater attention to their happiness.

So what should we do to increase the happiness of people with ID? According to the ancient Greek philosophers, the answer depends on our time frame: If we are interested in helping people with ID (whom I'll refer to throughout as "consumers") find happiness for today, we might serve them a good meal or throw them a party. If we are interested in helping them find happiness over the remainder of their lives, we need to schedule activities that provide deeper satisfactions than those derived from parties.

Notice how little overlap there is between what consumers need to do to maximize immediate versus lifespan happiness. These differences are so great I have distinguished two kinds of happiness (Reiss, 2000): "Feel-good happiness" refers to sensual pleasure, whereas "value-based happiness" refers to an enduring psychological sense that our life is meaningful. Although consumers need both kinds of happiness, value-based happiness is a more desirable goal because it produces much deeper and longer lasting satisfactions.

My point is that consumer happiness requires much more than a good time every now and then. It requires a life filled with purpose and experiences consumers value. To increase the happiness of a consumer, you need to learn about the individual's goals, dreams, and values.

This book includes practical suggestions on how to help consumers find value-based happiness. I have nothing against feel-good happiness: Adding fun to consumers' daily schedules is a good idea. Encouraging parents or caregivers to provide fun activities helps make life more pleasant for many consumers -- they can go on hay rides, visit amusement parks, or sing around campfires. A fun-filled life, however, isn't necessarily a meaningful life. In order to experience their lives as meaningful, consumers need purpose, meaning, and significance in addition to fun.

Feel-Good Happiness

Scholars concerned with feel-good happiness have endorsed the "Pleasure Principle," or the idea that happiness is a simple emotional sum of how often the individual has positive feelings minus how often the individual has negative feelings (see Eberstein, 1991). These scholars, called *hedonists*, advise consumers to take pleasure whenever they can because they do not know what might happen to them in the future. Maybe they will succumb to some illness or lose a valued caregiver. Perhaps a friend will move away or be assigned to a different residential unit. Maybe a loved one will die or become ill, or the consumer will be hurt in an accident. In such an uncertain world, say hedonists, consumers should live for today.

Aristippus (435 BCE – 366BCE) was among western philosophy's earliest advocates of pleasure theory (Irwin, 1995). His aim was to live life to its fullest: He advocated frequent partying, wine, sex, and feasts. He advised others to seek wealth and to maximize sensual pleasures.

Limitations of Feel-Good Happiness. A life of pleasure sounds good, but pleasure alone is not enough to sustain us. Philosophers have noted the following limitations on how much happiness one can derive from positive feeling states such as pleasure.

(1) Pleasure is short-lived. The pleasures of eating dissipate rapidly. Drunkenness is pleasurable for a few hours at most. Even the intense pleasures of love making quickly diminish upon sexual release.

(2) Pleasure obeys the law of diminishing returns. Thrills are easy to find at first, but pleasure seekers need increasingly adventurous pursuits in order to reach the same level of excitement. It is hard to find experiences that keep the thrills rolling hour after hour, day after day.

(3) The two different lifestyles based on the Pleasure Principle, which I call *self-indulgence* and *self-denial*, are contradictory. The goal of a self-indulgent lifestyle is to maximize the experience of sensual pleasures. In contrast, the goal of a lifestyle of self-denial is to minimize discomfort and suffering, to avoid such experiences as worry, fear, pain, sadness, and guilt. The problem with the Pleasure Principle is that you can live to maximize pleasure, or you can live to minimize pain, but you can't do both. So to be a hedonist, you must choose between a lifestyle of self-indulgence versus self-denial.

Nearly all hedonists of historical significance were self-deniers. In a world in which famine, war, plague, and injustice are common, the goal of minimizing suffering has had greater appeal than that of seeking sensual pleasures. Epicures (341 BCE – 270 BCE), for example, is one of history's best-remembered hedonists. He taught that the greatest goal in life is to minimize the experience of worry and pain (Inwood & Gerson, 1994). Although the popular version of "Epicureanism" is "eat, drink, and be merry, for tomorrow we die," he actually gave the opposite advice. Epicurus advised his followers to eat simply -- to avoid indigestion -- and to keep merriment to a minimum -- to avoid exhaustion. He embraced personal poverty as a means of avoiding the possible disappointments of losing one's wealth in an uncertain economy. When you do not own much, you will suffer neither the jealousy of neighbors nor much sadness when the stock market crashes. You should not worry about death because dead people feel no pain. Epicurus' philosophy was popular for 700 years.

Value-Based Happiness

As noted previously, value-based happiness is a sense that one's life is meaningful and fulfils a larger purpose than biological existence. We experience value-based happiness when we assert our values or embrace a lifestyle that meets our human needs.

We cannot experience value-based happiness by focusing on positive thoughts and feelings, as some psychologists have assumed. Instead, we must aim for satisfaction of needs and values. As J. S. Mill (1873) observed,

> I never ... wavered in the conviction that happiness is the test of all rules of conduct, and the end [goal] of life. But I now thought that this end was only to be attained by not making it the direct end. Those only are happy (I thought) who have their minds fixed on some object other than their own happiness; on the happiness of others, on the improvement of mankind, even on some art or pursuit, followed not as a means, but as itself an ideal end. Aiming at something else, they find happiness by the way. The enjoyments of life (such was now my theory) are sufficient to make it a pleasant thing, when they are taken *en passant,* without being made a principal object.

True happiness comes from satisfying our needs and core values. In order to increase our experience of value-based happiness, we need to become clear on who we are as individuals, identify our most important needs and values, and live our lives in ways that affirm our values and gratify our needs.

Because we have the potential to recall past meaningful experiences, value-based happiness is enduring. When we recall the birth of our children, we re-experience our love for them. When we recall a career success, we re-experience the power of having mastered something. The caregiver who recalls helping people reach independent living re-experiences the value-based happiness of serving others and watching them grow.

Unlike feel-good happiness, value-based happiness does not follow the law of diminishing returns. There are no limits on how meaningful a person's life can be. When we have an enduring feeling of this kind of happiness, we remain motivated to express our values and experience even more meaning.

We experience life as meaningless only when we are not true to our values or when we lose support from significant others. The loss of a loved one, for example, can lead to feelings of emptiness, despair, and meaninglessness. Loss of honor, freedom, or status also can cause significant unhappiness. Shame, too, is an indicator of loss of value-based happiness.

Value-Based Happiness and ID. In order to increase the value-based happiness among people with ID, we should help them experience the activities they most value. A person with ID who is gregarious, for example, has the potential to experience value-based happiness during social experiences, whereas a curious person has the potential to experience value-based happiness during learning experiences. A competitive person has the potential to experience value-based happiness by playing competitive games, whereas a willful person has the potential to experience value-based happiness when leading or influencing others.

Szymanski (2000) suggested that value-based happiness may be rooted in a positive self-concept. Crocker (2000) suggested that value-based happiness requires goals, social life, adequate rest, and leisure. In order to increase value-based happiness among people with ID, therefore, we should pay attention to their self-concept, life goals, values, and human needs.

One Size Does Not Make All Happy. When it comes to the experiences that produce value-based happiness, one size does not fit all. The same lifestyle may lead to value-based happiness, pleasantness, and a good quality of life for some, but unhappiness, unpleasantness, and a poor quality of life for others (Felce & Perry, 1996). Here are some common examples:

- Standing in the spotlight will make one person feel important but completely embarrass another.

- Taking care of children makes one person feel needed but makes another feel burdened and overwhelmed.

- Social activities are fun for gregarious people but tiring and stressful for private people.

So in helping consumers find value-based happiness, we need to help them become who they are, not who we want them to be. As Szymanski (2000) put it, "A most important caveat when assessing the quality of life/ adjustment/happiness of persons with mental retardation is to differenti- ate between their goals and views and those of the caregivers and profes- sionals involved."

Great Equalizer

Value-based happiness is the great equalizer in life. For example, the same feelings of achievement are experienced when a child with physical disabilities learns to walk as when a gifted athlete wins a sports competi- tion. The feelings are the same because each has met a significant person- al challenge. Further, the same feelings of intimacy and companionship are experienced when consumers fall in love as when intellectually gifted people fall in love. The same joy of friendship is experienced when con- sumers socialize with each other as when intellectually gifted students socialize with each other.

It is learning itself – not what is learned -- that produces value-based happiness for curious people. You do not have to be smart to enjoy learn- ing; you just need to have a thirst for learning. People with ID are not intel- lectually smart, but have the potential to enjoy learning (Reiss & Reiss, 2004).

Religious people say that everybody is equal before God. Certainly, everybody has an approximately equal opportunity to experience value- based happiness. Living in accordance with one's values lead to true hap- piness, and, since nearly everybody has the potential to do this, everybody should be able to experience value-based happiness.

Question: What do you have to do to experience value-based happiness?
Answer: Live your life in accordance with your own deeply held values. Be who you are, not who others want you to be.

Question: What does a consumer have to do to experience value-based happiness?
Answer: Live his/her life in accordance with his/her own deeply held values. Each must be who he/she is, not who some professional, advocate, or caregiver wants the person to be.

Conclusion

We need to pay more attention to the happiness of people with ID. Since happiness can be broken down into two kinds, pleasure (feel-good happiness) and meaning (value-based happiness), consumers need opportunities to experience both. In addition to providing opportunities for moderate degrees of fun and pleasure -- such as good meals, treats, fun experiences, sex, and the chance to experience beauty -- we should identify what each individual needs and values and offer activities that gratify these needs and express these values. Deep happiness is experienced when one's needs are met, not by having fun. In the remainder of this book, I offer practical methods for identifying a consumer's deepest needs.

Chapter 2

The Construct of Priorities

This chapter will present the conceptual foundations of my approach for assessing the human needs of consumers. Since portions of this chapter are rooted in academic philosophies of happiness, ethics, and choice, at times the discussion is rigorous. Some readers who are interested in simply applying my theory without understanding its foundations may wish to skip to Chapter 3 (research foundations) or even to Chapter 4 (practical implications for person-centered planning).

Recurring Nature of Needs

As I use them, the terms "life motive," "fundamental motive," "core motive," and "human need" are interchangeable. Psychologists have articulated a number of different ideas about fundamental motives. Freud (1963/1916), for example, discussed motivation as psychic *energy,* whereas Hull (1943) discussed motivation as a state of biological deprivation called *drive.* In contrast, I define motivation as the assertion of intrinsically held values, and I define motives as reasons for initiating or maintaining behavior.

I make no distinction between biological and psychological needs. Though many psychologists have drawn such distinctions, the similarities between so-called biological and psychological needs are much more important than the differences. I recognize both eating and social contact, for example, as human needs.

By definition, human needs are fundamental motives that can be satiated only temporarily. Hours or days after we satiate a need, it automatically regains strength and motivates us anew. Eating, for example, temporarily satiates our hunger, but we become hungry again not long afterward. Parties temporarily satiate our need for social contact, but we feel lonely again hours or days after the party is over and we have spent time being alone.

Since life motives invariably recur, they influence our behavior over the entire lifespan (hence, the term *life motive*). The need for social contact, for example, motivates social behavior from cradle to tomb. Similarly, the need to help others motivates altruism over the lifespan.

Intrinsic Motivation

Aristotle (1953/330 BCE) distinguished between *intrinsic* and *instrumental* goals. Intrinsic goals are what we want; instrumental goals are the means we use to obtain what we want. Gratifying a need (such as eating and social contact) is an intrinsic goal. Human activities that enable needs to be gratified are instrumental goals. Playing softball, for example, is a common instrumental motive to obtain the intrinsically-valued goal of physical activity. Reading a book is a common instrumental motive for experiencing the intrinsic goal of learning.

A series of instrumental goals can create a behavior chain that leads to one or more intrinsically valued goals. A young woman with ID may take a bus to a local McDonald's fast food restaurant; work at the McDonald's; earn pay; and feel competent and self-reliant because she has a paying job. In this example, riding the bus, working, and seeking pay all are instrumental activities motivated by the intrinsically-valued goals of competence and self-reliance. These intrinsic goals motivate the entire chain of behavior: If the individual did not hold these intrinsically valued goals, none of the behaviors would occur.

Intrinsic Values

Human needs and intrinsically held values are so closely connected to each other we can infer one from the other and vice versa. The need for physical activity, for example, motivates people to value fitness, whereas the need for independence motivates people to value self-determination.

Needs also indicate the purpose, or the meaning, of behavior. The purpose of physical activity, for example, is to satisfy the need for muscle exercise. The purpose of avoiding criticism is to gratify the need for acceptance.

Universal Motives

Human needs motivate everybody. As McDougall (2003/1908) put it,

> Every man is so constituted to seek, to strive for, and to desire certain goals which are common to the species, and the attainment of which goals satisfies and allays the cravings or desire that move us. These goals... are not only common to all men, but also ... [to] their nearer relatives in the animal world; such goals as food, shelter from danger, the company of our fellows, intimacy with the opposite sex, triumph over our opponents, and leadership among our companions.

The first influential psychologists to study human needs were the "instinct theorists." In the late 19th century, for example, William James (1918/1890) identified the following as basic human instincts: imitation, aggression, socializing, helping others, hunting, fear, collecting, making things, play, curiosity, secretiveness, cleanliness, sex, parenting, and jealousy.

In the first decade of the 20th century, William McDougall (2003/1908) argued that there are 12 principal instincts of human nature. These were flight, repulsion, curiosity, aggression, attention-seeking, submission, child rearing, reproduction, eating, socializing, collecting, and making things.

Henry A. Murray (1938) substituted the construct of psychological or human need for that of instinct. His list of 27 needs was similar to previous lists of instincts and became influential in part because he applied them to clinical assessment.

Although many other lists of psychological needs have been suggested, the various lists are generally similar (Reiss, 2008, pp. 22-36): In alphabetical order, Reiss's (2008) 16 human needs are acceptance, curiosity, eating, family, honor, idealism, independence, order, physical activity, power, romance, saving, social contact, status, tranquility, and vengeance.

Regulation of Life Motives

Each individual has an optimal level for experiencing each human need. For "vengeance," for example, one person may be happiest embracing confrontation while another is happiest avoiding it. For "Learning," one person may be happiest spending hours on educational tasks, while another may prefer to spend only a few minutes at a time.

People are motivated to regulate and balance their behavior to avoid the twin displeasures of excess and insufficiency. What is "too much" and "too little" depends on the individual's optimal levels for experiencing each need. In Figure 2-1, for example, we see the degree to which Henry and Jake differ in optimal levels for the need for social contact. Henry seeks peer companionship about 10 percent of his waking hours, whereas Jake has a much higher optimal level for socializing and seeks peer companionship about 50 percent of his day. When Henry and Jake experience more social contact than they desire, they are temporarily motivated to avoid socializing. When they experience less social contact than they desire, they are motivated to socialize. When the amount of social contact they experience is about what they desire, they are temporarily satiated in their desire for social contact.

Suppose that Henry and Jake attend a party that lasts three hours.

Henry enjoys the party at first, but after a while the continued demand to socialize drains his energy. Jake, on the other hand, is full of pep when the party ends. After the party, Henry goes home for quiet time and rest, whereas Jake and friends go to the nearest bar to keep the party rolling.

Figure 2-1. Two Optimal Levels of the Human Need for Social Contact

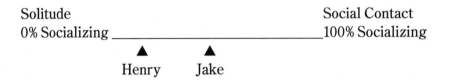

People regulate, moderate, and balance their experiences to match their optimal levels. At the same time, the regulatory processes are imprecise and approximate. A person might aim to exercise about one hour per day. On any given day, however, he or she may spend significantly more or less time engaged in physical activity and might even go a week or two without exercise. But over the course of his or her life, however, the prioritization of physical activity will remain stable relative to his/her age cohort.

Individual Priorities

Optimal levels can be considered as expressing priorities and intrinsically held values. In Figure 2-1, we might say that Jake gives a higher priority to social contact than does Henry, and that Jake intrinsically values social life more than does Henry.

This analysis suggests that human needs have two elements, *universal reinforcing stimulus* and *priority*, with priority indicating the value a person places on a universally reinforcing stimulus. Everybody has a need for acceptance, but some people prioritize this need much more highly than do others. Everybody has a need for order, but some people prioritize this need much more highly than do others.

The same human needs motivate various people in different ways. The need for vengeance, for example, motivates people with a high optimal level to embrace competitive activities, while motivating people with a low optimal level to embrace cooperative behavior. The need for tranquility motivates people with a high optimal level to embrace safety, while motivating people with a low optimal level optimal level to embrace adventure.

In other words, the same universally reinforcing stimuli motivate various people quite differently. Orderliness is universally reinforcing in the sense that nobody is indifferent to how organized their environment or schedule is. Yet some people are motivated to embrace high degrees of orderliness, while others are motivated to embrace low degrees of orderliness. Human suffering is a universally reinforcing stimulus that motivates some to help and others to look the other way. In order to understand what makes people happy, we need to know what are universally reinforcing stimuli for all humanity and the range of individual prioritizations and reactions of such stimuli.

Objections to Motivation Theory

The influence of previous theories of human needs have been effectively limited by numerous criticisms made by rival psychologists. Although some of these criticisms may have had merit when they were raised with regard to their original subjects, they do not apply to this new approach to human needs.

Explanatory Fictions. Many behaviorists are suspicious of the explanatory status of motivational constructs (Skinner, 1938). They think motivational theorists infer states (e.g., hunger) from observations of behavior (e.g., eating), only to explain behavior (e.g., eating) in terms of the inferred motivational state (e.g., hunger). The dog ate because he was hungry, and we know the dog was hungry because he ate. Skinner (1938) called such analyses "explanatory fictions." He held that explanatory, motivational constructs must be tied to observable phenomena, both antecedent (e.g., time elapsed since last consumption of food) and consequent variables (e.g., organism scans environment searching for food).

While "explanatory fictions" may well apply to theories of state motives, they do not apply to human needs (life motives). Suppose a researcher notices that a particular horse, Speedy Charlie, eats much more food than other horses over a period of time and, based on such observations, infers that Speedy Charlie has a particularly strong "need" for eating. The horse ate because he is a glutton, and I know the horse is a glutton because in the past I repeatedly observed him consuming more food than other horses. This explanatory statement is not circular because it predicts that behavior (higher than average food consumption) occurring today or over a recent period is likely to be observable many weeks, months, or even years into the future. The prediction isn't obvious: Skinnerian theorists may deny the prediction because they believe the future rate of Speedy Charlie's eating will depend on unknown, future reinforcement contingencies.

While it is circular to say that Smith is asking questions because he is curious and I know he is curious because he is asking questions, it is not circular to infer trait curiosity from observations of current inquiring behavior and to predict above-average rates of inquiring behavior in the future. Such predictions are falsifiable and not obvious. Behaviorists say, for example, that future inquiring behavior cannot be predicted without knowledge of future reinforcement contingencies. Yet needs analysis predicts future behavior without knowledge of future reinforcement contingencies. These predictions may turn out to be invalid, but they are not circular.

Motivational needs are not explanatory fictions; self-reports are not explanatory fictions (Malcolm, 1966). If two people were vengeful, for example, Reiss's (2008) theory of 16 psychological needs would predict that the person who places above-average valuation on honor is less likely to "act out" the vengeance than is the individual who places below-average valuation on honor. You may disagree with these predictions, but to say the predictions are based on circular logic would be invalid.

Drive/Instinct Naming. Motivation theory has been criticized for "instinct naming" and "drive naming." Critics asserted that motivational theorists arbitrarily invented new drives, instincts, or needs for nearly every human goal (Dunlap, 1919; Hunt, 1971; Murphy, 1929; Woodworth, 1928). The seemingly arbitrary way instincts and drives were recognized, plus the sheer number of such motives, led many behavioral scientists to reject needs analysis as unscientific.

By objectively constructing and then validating taxonomies of human needs, we avoid the historical problem of arbitrarily naming drives and instincts. Reiss and Havercamp (1998), for example, submitted motivation questionnaire data to a series of factor analyses (research discussed in Chapter 3). The results showed 15 factors that were subsequently validated by a separate confirmatory factor study with new samples. When colleagues suggested a sixteenth human need, called saving, the questionnaire was expanded, and new confirmatory factor studies were successfully executed. Each of the 16 human needs was subsequently shown to predict the results of other, previously validated psychological scales and/or real-world behavior, including future behavior in natural environments (Reiss, 2008, pp 25-28). The 16 needs have remained unchanged for more than eight years of further research, during which time they were applied to personality theory (Olson & Webber, 2004), relationships (Engel, Olson, & Patrick, 2002; Judah, 2006; Wiltz & Reiss, 2003), sports (Reiss, Wiltz, & Sherman, 2001) and spirituality (Reiss, 2004b). Regardless of whether or not one accepts the taxonomy of 16 human needs, it can't be dismissed as mere "drive-naming" because it was empirically derived and validated (Havercamp & Reiss, 2003).

When Reiss expanded his taxonomy from 15 to 16 needs, some critics asserted that is was an instance of drive naming (e.g., Freeman, Anderson, Azer, Girolami, & Scotti, 1998). Chemistry's Periodic Table of Elements has been expanded many times, yet nobody argues that chemistry is not "scientific." If chemists can keep adding to their taxonomy of fundamental elements, surely behavioral scientists can recognize a sixteenth human need.

The criticism that motivation theorists have identified "too many" human needs is invalid; there is no number favored in science other than the number observed in nature. Needs theorists have generated taxonomies of anywhere from six to 27 life motives (Reiss, 2000a, 2008). Chemists recognize 118 elements, biologists recognize millions of cells in the human body, and physicists say the universe has billions of heavenly bodies. Nobody criticizes chemists, biologists, and physicists for studying "too many" elements, cells, or objects.

Conclusion

To help consumers experience a better quality of life with greater happiness, we need to help them satisfy their most important human needs. First, we should identify or list out the human needs of people with ID. Next, we need to assess the individual's priorities (or hierarchy of needs). Finally, we should schedule activities that regularly satisfy the individual's most important needs.

Human needs motivate everybody but not in the same way. The need for order, for example, motivates everybody, but order motivates some people to organize and others to seek spontaneity. The need for learning motivates everybody, but this need motivates some people to value ideas and others to value practical actions. To apply our knowledge of human needs to assist consumers, we need to understand how each human need motivates each individual. The methods presented in this book will show you how to do this.

The human needs discussed in this book were empirically derived and validated. These needs cannot be criticized as "explanatory fictions" or arbitrarily named drives.

Chapter 3

Twelve Needs Relevant to People with Intellectual Disabilities

What do people with ID want from life? Do they want the same experiences everybody wants? What goals and strivings make their lives meaningful and give purpose to their behavior? After more than a decade of scientific research and professional experience, we have made significant progress addressing these important questions. In this chapter we will review our work on the assessment and implications of human needs in the general population, and then we will consider the results of our effort to study such needs with people with ID.

Reiss Motivation Profile (RMP)

Throughout history scholars have put forth theories of human needs based on philosophical inquiries, observations of animals, behavioral observations, and personal experiences. In 1995 I began to study scientifically what makes life meaningful. I asked thousands of people from diverse walks in life what motivates them. The chief result of our research, first published in Reiss and Havercamp (1998), appears to be the first empirically derived taxonomy of human needs.

My current version of what motivates people, based on a standardized questionnaire called the Reiss Motivational Profile (RMP), identifies the following 16 human needs.

Acceptance, the need for approval
Curiosity, the need to learn
Eating, the need for food
Family, the need for family bonding
Honor, the need to behave according to a moral code
Idealism, the need to improve society
Independence, the need for self-reliance
Order, the need for orderliness
Physical activity, the need for muscle exercise

Power, the need for influence
Romance, the need for sex
Saving, the need to collect
Social Contact, the need for peer companionship
Status, the need be an important person
Tranquility, the need for safety
Vengeance, the need to get even with those who frustrate or offend

The RMP is a 128-item, standardized questionnaire that assesses how an individual prioritizes the 16 human needs (Reiss, 2008). Each item on the instrument is meant to measure the strength of an individual's life motive. The item stems consist of the phrases, "I like," "I enjoy," "I am happiest when," "I love, "I try," "I must have," "I hate," "I am proud of," "I want," and "is important to me." Some examples of items included, "I love to eat," "Sex is very important to me," "I am happiest when I am physically active," and "I love parties."

Empirical Derivation. The 128-item RMP was empirically derived. When the research began, there were 328 test items, now known as RMP Iteration I. Reiss and Havercamp (1998) administered this questionnaire to hundreds of volunteers; submitted the results to factor analysis; and then revised the questionnaire. The revised questionnaire, now known as RMP Iteration II, was administered to a new group of volunteers. The process of factor analysis and instrument revision was repeated three times and followed with a fourth, confirmatory factor study. Each RMP iteration was administered to a different sample of people and no one participated in more than one study. The samples consisted of 401, 380, 341, and 398 people, respectively, and all of them included adolescents and adults from diverse walks in life and various states of residence. The fourth study confirmed the 15-factor solution. Subsequently, we executed factor analytic research intended to add a sixteenth factor, called Saving, to assess the motive of hoarding. Havercamp (1998) confirmed the 16-factor solution with a new sample of 512 adults solicited from several sources in urban and rural Ohio and Indiana.

Throughout our research, human needs found to have little or no relevance for psychology – primarily certain biological needs – were deleted[1]. Thirst is such a life motive: How much water we drink has almost nothing to do with our values, personality, or life goals and by excluding it, I significantly shortened my theory with minimal loss of relevance. [1]

---

[1] Significance is also a determinant in taxonomies in the physical sciences. Not everything that orbits the Sun, for example, is regarded as a planet —Pluto's recent "demotion" to Kuiper Belt Object being a well-known case in point – because the great bulk of the lengthy list of every identifiable rock or substance in the solar system has only the most minor significance with the science of astronomy.

Reliability. We assessed the four-week, test-retest reliabilities obtained from a sample of 123 racially diverse, undergraduate students. The Pearson product-moment correlations ranged from .69 to .88 (M = .80). These results can be compared to those reported for other personality assessments. Hjelle and Bernard (1994), for example, reported 3-week test-retest reliabilities ranging from .32 to .78 (M = .60) across the subscales of the Personality Research Form (PRF; Jackson, 1984). Test-retest reliability coefficients over the course of a 1-week interval for the Minnesota Multiphasic Personality Inventory-2 (Butcher, Dahlstrom. Graham, Tellegen, & Kaemmer, 1989), were .58 to .92, with an average of .79, for the various MMPI scales. These findings suggest that the RMP scales have a test-retest reliability comparable to that associated with other widely-used personality tests.

We estimated internal reliabilities from two data sets, one of which was a sample of 398 racially diverse adolescents and adults (see Study 4 in Reiss and Havercamp, 1998). These alpha coefficients ranged from .74 to .92, with a median of .82. The other data set was from a sample of 171 racially diverse undergraduate students (Havercamp & Reiss, 2003). These alpha coefficients ranged from .79 to .94 with a median of .88. These findings suggest that the RMP scales have internal reliability comparable to that associated with widely-used personality tests.

Social Desirability. In order to estimate the degree to which individuals give answers they think make them look good, we assessed the social desirability of the RMP scales (Havercamp & Reiss, 2003). The correlations between the RMP's 16 scales and the Marlowe-Crowne Social Desirability Scale ranged in absolute value from .01 to .39 (M = .16). By comparison, Jackson (1984) reported correlations between social desirability and content for the PRF as ranging from .01 to .44 (M= .22). These findings suggest that the RMP scales are minimally affected by social desirability.

Concurrent Validity. The RMP scales are significantly correlated with NEO-P-I-R (Big 5; Costa & McCrae, 1992); Myers Briggs Type Indicator (MBTI; Myers, McCaulley, Quenk, & Hammer, 1998); Work Preference Inventory measure of intrinsic and extrinsic motivation (Amabile, Hill, Hennessey, & Tighe, 1994); Purpose in Life (Crumbaugh & Maholick, 1964); self-efficacy in choosing a career (Betz, Klein, & Taylor, 1996); Personality Research Form (Jackson, 1984); Sternberg Triangular Love Scale (Sternberg, 1998); Relationship Assessment Scale (Hendrick, 1988), and Anxiety Sensitivity Index (Reiss, Peterson, Taylor, Schmidt, & Weems, 2008). These findings provide evidence for the concurrent validity of the RMP scales.

Criterion Validity. Researchers have demonstrated that the 16 RMP scales for assessing human needs are associated with the following psychological criterion outcomes.

1. Personality (Havercamp & Reiss, 2003; Olson & Weber, 2004)
2. Membership in various interest groups (Havercamp & Reiss, 2003)
3. Psychopathology (Olson & Weber, 2004)
4. Spirituality (Beasley and Rowell, 2002; Reiss, 2000b)
5. Relationships (Engel, Olson, & Patrick, 2002)
6. Athletic performance (Reiss, Wiltz, & Sherman, 2001)
7. Television viewing (Reiss and Wiltz, 2004)
8. Adult age (Reiss & Havercamp, 2005)
9. Organ donor card status (Reiss and Crouch (2005)
10. Intrinsic and extrinsic motivation (Olson & Chapin 2007)
11. Grades in high school (Kavanaugh & Reiss, 2001)

These findings provide evidence for the criterion validity of the RMP scales (see Reiss, 2008 for summary of the results of 17 studies).

Reiss Motivation Profile MR/DD

Since the RMP is a questionnaire, it is suitable only for individuals who can understand the items. For individuals with ID who can understand the questions but are not able to read, facilitators can read aloud the items and record the responses. For those with ID who cannot understand the items, a version of the RMP, the Reiss Profile Mental Retardation/ Developmental Disabilities (RMP-MR/DD), was constructed.

Empirical Derivation. The RMP-MR/DD is an empirically derived rating scale that is completed by caregivers, parents, or teachers. The RMP-MR/DD Iteration I consisted of 157 items intended to assess 10 life motives: anxiety sensitivity, attention seeking, eating, frustration sensitivity, helps others, independence, order, physical exercise, positive mood, and social contact (Reiss & Havercamp, 1998). About two-thirds of the items directly referred to motives, such as "More than most people, seeks attention," and "Always wants to win." Some items were written to refer to behaviors that strongly implied, but did not explicitly describe, motivation.

At a national conference on dual diagnosis (mental illness and mental retardation), professionals and parents rated 199 people with MR/DD. Steven Reiss used the inter-item correlation matrix to develop a 162-item revised instrument, called RMP-MR/DD Iteration II. This instrument included items intended to assess 15 life motives -- the original 10 minus positive mood, but plus curiosity, morality, pain sensitivity, acceptance, romance, and vengeance.

Reiss and Havercamp (1998) administered the 162-item RMP-MR/ DD to 515 people (304 men and 211 women). The age distribution was 14.6 percent for age group 0-21, 75.5 percent for those 22-55, and 9.9 percent for those 56 or over. The percentage racial composition was 20.8 African American, 1.2 percent Asian American, 75.2 percent Caucasian, and 2.8 percent Hispanic. All levels of intellectual disabilities -- mild (n=249), moderate (n=137), and severe/profound (n=107) -- were represented. The sample included 166 people without behavior disorders and 346 people with them. The sample and their raters were recruited from eight community-based service and residential agencies located in Massachusetts, Connecticut, Pennsylvania, Ontario, Illinois, Texas, Ohio, and the United Kingdom. The raters were limited to those who said they had known the person they were rating for at least four months. In order to limit the extent to which the results might be influenced by a single rater, none of them rated more than one consumer. The raters were also asked to indicate whether the participants had been identified previously as having a behavior disorder.

The ratings were submitted to a series of exploratory factor analyses using the maximum likelihood extraction method with oblique rotations. The first analysis extracted 10 factors, the second 11, and so on up to 20 factors. Because the factor loadings for the 20-factor solution were very small, further analyses were not conducted. The 14-factor solution was the easiest to interpret; the solution accounted for 52% of the variance. Even though a scale for social contact did not emerge from the exploratory factor analysis, it was retained anyway because of its theoretical importance for people with ID. We then used the analysis to pare the number of items and interpret 15 factors, which became the 15 scales of RMP-MR/DD Iteration III.

Reiss and Havercamp (1998) conducted a confirmatory factor study on the RMP- MR/DD Iteration III. The sample consisted of 438 people (248 men, 189 women, 1 unreported) from 24 states. Staff or relatives who attended a research presentation at the 1996 national meeting of the Arc of the United States were asked to provide ratings. Other raters provided services at a large residential agency with headquarters in Ohio, a large residential provider of group homes in suburban Chicago, or a residential dual diagnosis program near Philadelphia. The percentage age distribution was 10.2 for participants aged 0-21, 78.2 for those 22-55, and 11.6 for those 56 and older. Twenty-five percent were African American, 75 percent Caucasian. The intellectual disabilities severity levels were mild (n=250), moderate (n=137), and severe/profound (n=107). The sample included 250 people with a behavior disorder and 179 people with no behavior disorder. When we allowed the factors to correlate, the 15-factor solution provided a reasonable fit to the data, RMSEA = .078, which is evidence of the factorial validity of the RMP-MR/DD.

The current RMP-MR/DD ratings instrument assesses the following 15 human needs, most corresponding to those in the general RMP but redefined to have greater relevance to the ID population:

Acceptance is the need to avoid criticism.
Attention is the need for notice.
Curiosity is the need for knowledge.
Eating is the need to consume food.
Helps Others is the need for altruism.
Independence is the need for self-reliance.
Morality is the need to do what the individual was taught is right.
Order is the need for organization.
Physical activity is the need for muscle exercise.
Romance is the need for sex.
Social contact is the need for peer companionship.
Anxiety (Tranquility I) is the need to be free of anxiety and stress.
Frustration (Tranquility II) is the need to be free of frustration.
Pain (Tranquility III) is the need to be free of pain.
Vengeance is the need to get even with those who offend.

Lecavalier and Tasse (2001) translated, adapted, and validated the Reiss Profile MR/DD on a sample of 588 French-Canadian adolescents and adults with ID. The ratings were submitted to confirmatory factor analysis and yielded an RMSEA of .079, indicating a reasonable fit to the Reiss and Havercamp (1998) model. For the 15 scales, the mean alpha coefficient of internal reliability was .84, and the mean inter-rater correlation was .63.

Reliability. Reiss and Havercamp (1998) conducted an assessment of test-retest reliability over a three-week period. The sample consisted of 44 individuals (21 men and 23 women) receiving services from a large not-for-profit ID service agency with headquarters in New York. Their ages ranged from 22 to 79; racial composition was 86% Caucasian and 14% African American. Seventy percent were reported to have a behavior disorder. Agency psychology staff and direct care workers were the raters for the instrument. The r values for the 15 scales ranged from .72 to .89, with a mean of .81, which is evidence of the stability of the scale scores over time.

Lecavalier and Havercamp (2004) demonstrated the stability of the 15 RMP-MR/DD scores for 79 individuals over an approximate three-year time period. In this study, the test-retest reliability estimates were statistically significant for all 15 scales. Further, 89 percent of the raters could identify the person by examining the individual's profile.

Validity. Table 3-1 summarizes the evidence for the reliability and validity for each scale of the RMP, with FV indicating confirmed favor validity (each "✓" indicates a study successfully confirming factor validity).

Table 3-1. Reliability and Validity of Reiss Motivation Profile MR/DD

Scale	FV	r	α	Validity Evidence
Acceptance	✓	.73	.86	(1) People with acting out, aggressive or violent behavior scored significantly higher than those described as quiet (e.g., Crocker, Mercier, Allaire, & Roy, 2007). (2) Correlated with the Reiss Screen for Maladaptive Behavior, r = .37 (Lecavalier & Tasse, 2002). (3) Compatible roommates scored lower than incompatible roommates (Wiltz & Reiss, 2003).
Attention	✓	.82	.84	People with acting out, aggressive or violent behavior scored significantly higher than those described as quiet (e.g., Crocker, Mercier, Allaire, & Roy, 2007).
Curiosity	✓	.72	.82	(1) Prospectively predicted quality of life six months after testing, r = .28 (Lunsky, 1999). (2) Males with Klinefelter syndrome scored high on self report assessment (Gerschwind & Dykens, 2004). (3) Students with reputation for curiosity scored very high (Reiss & Reiss, 2004)
Eating	✓	.89	.90	(1) People with Prader Willi syndrome scored very high for RMP-MR/DD eating (Dykens & Rosener, 1999). (2) People with Down syndrome scored high (Lecavalier & Tasse, 2005).

Helps Others	✓	.81	.89	(1) People with aggressive or violent behavior scored significantly lower than those described as quiet (e.g., Crocker, Mercier, Allaire, & Roy, 2007). (2) People with a dual diagnosis scored low on RMP-MR/DD Helps Others.
Independence	✓	.82	.83	Face validity of items.
Morality	✓	.82	.69	(1) People with acting out, aggressive or violent behavior scored significantly lower than those described as quiet (e.g., Crocker, Mercier, Allaire, & Roy, 2007). (2) Males with Klinefelter syndrome scored high on self report assessment (Gerschwind & Dykens, 2004).
Order	✓	.82	.81	(1) People with Prader Willi and Williams syndrome scored high (Dykens & Rosener, 1999). (2) Compatible roommates scored lower than incompatible roommates (Wiltz & Reiss, 2003).
Physical Activity	✓	.79	.83	Predicted quality of life 6-months after testing, r = .24.
Romance	✓	.83	.88	Face validity of items.
Social Contact	✓	.78	.80	(1) People with autism scored very low on RMP-MR/DD social contact (Lunsky, 1999). (2) High scores predicted quality of life six months later (Lunsky, 1999). (3) Males with Klinefelter syndrome scored high on self report assessment (Gerschwind & Dykens, 2004). (4) People matched on RMP-MR/DD social contact more likely to become friends (Wiltz & Kalnins, 2008).

Anxiety (Tranquility I)	✓	.83	.77	(1) Low scores predicted quality of life six months after testing, r=-.49 (Lunsky, 1999). (2) People with a dual diagnosis scored high, r=.50 (Lecavalier & Tasse, 2002). (3) People with autism scored high (Lunsky, 1999). (4) Compatible roommates scored lower than incompatible roommates (Wiltz & Reiss, 2003).
Frustration (Tranquility II)	✓	.82	.88	(1) People with acting out, aggressive, or violent behavior scored higher than those described as quiet (e.g., Crocker, Mercier, Allaire, & Roy, 2007). (2) People with a dual diagnosis scored high on RMP-MR/DD Frustration, r = .46 (Lecavalier & Tasse, 2002). (3) People with Down syndrome scored low (Lecavalier & Tasse, 2005). (4) Compatible roommates scored lower than incompatible roommates (Wiltz & Reiss, 2003).
Pain Sensitivity (Tranquility III)	✓	.79	.85	(1) People with acting out, aggressive, or violent behavior scored significantly higher than those described as quiet (e.g., Crocker, Mercier, Allaire, & Roy, 2007). (2) People with high total scores on the Reiss Screen for Maladaptive Behavior scored high for RMP MR/DD Pain, r = .37 (Lecavalier & Tasse, 2002). (3) People with Down syndrome scored low (Lecavalier & Tasse, 2005)

Vengeance	✓	.85	.90	(1) People with high total scores on the Reiss Screen for Maladaptive Behavior scored high on RMP- MR/DD vengeance (Lecavalier & Tasse, 2002). (2) People with acting out, aggressive, or violent behavior scored significantly higher than those described as quiet (e.g., Crocker, Mercier, Allaire, & Roy, 2007). (3) People with Prader Willi syndrome and those with Williams syndrome scored high on RMP MR/DD vengeance (Dykens & Rosner, 1999). (4) Compatible roommates scored lower than incompatible roommates (Wiltz & Reiss, 2003). (5) People with high scores are unfriendly (Wiltz & Kalnins, 2008).

Since the RMP-MR/DD was published in 2002, it has been used in developmental disabilities agencies throughout North America. Feedback about its usefulness has been positive.

Reiss Profile of Psychological Needs (RMP-ID)

In 2009 I sought to create a new instrument, called the *Reiss Profile of Psychological Needs* (RMP-ID), aimed at making the assessment of human needs more relevant to person-centered planning and crisis intervention. The initial psychometric research was executed with 299 participants from three states (Ohio, Michigan, and California), who were either caregivers or parents. The ratings were submitted to statistical analyses to determine the final list of items, scoring methods, and initial norms. In the fall of 2009 the "beta version" RMP-ID was made available for Internet administrations and additional research. The newer RMP-ID is a 60-item ratings scale that assesses the following 12 human needs.

Need for Acceptance is the need to avoid criticism.
Need for Attention is the need to be worthy of notice by others.
Need to Eat is the need to consume food.
Need to Help Others is the need for altruism.
Need for Independence is the need for self-reliance.
Need for Learning is the need for knowledge.

Need for Order is the need for organization.
Need for Physical Activity is the need for muscle exercise.
Need for Romance is the need for sex.
Need for Social Contact is the need for peer companionship.
Need for Tranquility is the need to avoid feared or painful stimuli.
Life Motive of Vengeance is the need to get even with those who offend.

Table 3-2 presents a comparison of three versions of the RMP. The newer RMP ID consolidates the three tranquility scales of the RMP-MR/DD into a single scale called "Tranquility" and combines the RMP-MR/DD scales for "Helps Others" and "Morality" into a single scale called "Helps Others." The RMP-ID does not include a scale for achievement motivation (which falls under RMP Power) because, for the vast majority of students with ID, to achieve means to do well in school (which falls under the Need to Learn).

Table 3-2. Comparison of RMP Versions

ID Version (60 items)	MR/DD Version (100 items)	General Population Version (128 items)
Acceptance	Acceptance	Acceptance
Attention	Attention	Status, Power
Eating	Eating	Eating
Helps Others	Helps Others	Family+ Idealism + Honor
Independence	Independence	Independence
Learning	Curiosity	Curiosity
Order	Order	Order
Physical Activity	Physical Activity	Physical Activity
Romance	Romance	Romance
Social Contact	Social Contact	Social Contact
Tranquility	Tranquility I + II +III	Tranquility
Vengeance	Vengeance	Vengeance

Conclusion

The RMP has proven to be a reliable and valid psychological questionnaire for assessing an individual's priorities for 16 human needs, a taxonomy that was empirically derived from the results of research on wide-ranging samples drawn from the general population. The instrument has internal and test-retest reliabilities comparable or slightly superior to those for widely-used comprehensive personality instruments and its factorial validity has been repeatedly confirmed. Concurrent, criterion, and social validity have been demonstrated, and the instrument has been used successfully in a number of research studies.

My work on human needs is available in two prior books: *Who Am I* (Reiss, 2000), which describes the research leading to the validation of the 16 human needs, and *Normal Personality: A New Way of Thinking about People* (Reiss, 2008), which describes the scholarship linking human needs and personality.

The present book discusses how the RMP-MR/DD, and the newer RMP-ID, can be used in the supervision and care of people with ID. The RMP ID is specifically intended to connect human needs to person centered planning and to dual diagnosis, including the prevention of violence and crisis intervention.

Chapter 4

Assessing Preferred Lifestyle

Person-centered Planning (PCP) refers to a variety of methods aimed at empowering individuals with ID to choose their own lifestyle (Holburn & Vietze, 2002; O'Brien & O'Brien, 2002). PCP variants include whole life planning (Butterworth, Hagner, Hikkinen, De Mello, & McDonough, 1993; O'Brien, 1987), personal futures planning (Mount, 1994; Mount & Zwenik, 1988), essential lifestyle planning (Smull & Harrison, 1992), and the PICTURE method (Holburn, Gordon, & Vietze, 2007). No one approach is recognized as superior to the others.

PCP requires a facilitator with exceptional people skills who spends time with the individual to learn about his/her values, preferences, and dreams. The facilitator convenes a meeting of the individual's planning group, which typically includes the individual, family, friends, and caregivers. Together they plan a supported lifestyle, school curriculum, transition from school to workplace, supported employment, housing, positive behavior supports, assisted technology, and any other needed supports (Butterworth, Whitney-Thomas, & Steere, 1997).

The goals of PCP are consistent with today's positive psychology movement. For example, people attending a PCP planning session are asked about the individual's greatest gifts, abilities, dreams, and aspirations. Some facilitators prohibit negative comments during planning sessions. The aim is to promote an appealing reputation for the individual and to counteract any negative or severe reputations.

The PICTURE method (Holburn et al., 2007) has the advantage of providing facilitators with details on how to conduct a PCP session. The team is asked to review eight areas of the individual's life: home, places, competence, respect, health, work, choices, and relationships. In each of these life areas, the team discussion is meant to focus on how things are currently versus how they should be in the future.

Challenges of PCP Interviewing

PCP facilitators use conversation to assess consumer goals. They ask questions such as, "What are your hopes and aspirations, and what can be done to help you achieve these." Although I support the general goals of PCP, I take issue with PCP's assumption that people know what they want out of life. When I was in my youth, for example, I was not very clear in my own mind as to what I wanted. Many people, especially young adults and adolescents, do not know what they want from life.

PCP planners may overestimate a person's self-knowledge. Any number of us cannot say what would truly make us happier. Some think, for example, that wealth brings happiness, but the results of large-scale studies suggest otherwise. Others think that success is the key to happiness, but there are many successful people who are unhappy. Every day people marry thinking they have found true love only to divorce a few years later. A person needs self-awareness, mentoring, knowledge, and experience to make valid choices; otherwise, choices can lead to unhappy mistakes. If ordinary people have trouble knowing who or what would make them happy, why should we assume that people with ID have such self-knowledge?

Many consumers do not know what they want from life. Like the rest of us, they may not know which work activities will produce enduring satisfaction or where they would most enjoy living. They may not know who to choose as roommates or how to schedule their time for a happy life.

Unlike us, once they have self determined their future, consumers cannot easily change their minds. If I move to a neighborhood but later discover I don't enjoy living there, I can move. Because of their reliance on government or family funding, however, consumers become "locked into" such decisions. It is imperative, therefore, that every tool be deployed to minimize errors during PCP sessions.

Self-awareness facilitates self-determination (Wehmeyer, Kelchner, & Richards, 1996). Psychologists have developed a variety of tools -- such as the Myers Briggs Type Indicator personality assessment (MBTI ; Myers et al., 1998) and the Reiss Motivation Profile (RMP; see Chapter 3) -- that are used to enhance self-awareness. Of these, only the RMP has been adapted for ID. Incorporating the results of the RMP can add objectivity to the PCP process by providing a measure of the consumer's intrinsically held values and life goals, information that should help reduce the number of unhappy choices consumers or planners mistakenly make.

Self-Hugging

PCP does not always work as intended. Planners recognize the problem of bias, in which planners misperceive their own values for those of individual consumers. Sometimes the consumer's views are ignored or consciously or unconsciously reinterpreted by the facilitator or by other members of the PCP committee.

"Self-hugging" is a natural tendency to impose our own values on others, thinking it is for the other person's own good (Reiss, 2000, 2008).

We all self-hug, and we do it often. Many parents, for example, impose their values on their children in the mistaken belief that they are acting in their child's best interests. An ambitious mother, for example, may think her children will be happiest if they are achieving. An athletic father may think his adult children should work out often. The children, of course, have a mind of their own and may fight for their independence once they become old enough to do so.

Self-hugging can motivate facilitators and planners to impose their values on consumers. Planners who value orderliness, for example, may assume that an organized lifestyle is best for all consumers. Facilitators who are athletic may assume that an active lifestyle is best for everyone. Planners who are timid may assume that all consumers should minimize risk and adventure. Such biases potentially undermine the goals of self-determination.

Many parents, caregivers, and professionals who impose their values on consumers are motivated by altruism. A gentle parent, having always experienced the competitive instinct as unpleasant, cannot imagine how any child could be truly happy participating in competitions. A competitive parent for whom the idea of backing down is shameful, by contrast, may not understand how their children could be happy walking away from fights.

Self-hugging PCP planners might unwittingly create an "everyday tyranny" in which consumers must live in accordance with values they do not really hold but are falsely asserted to have chosen. Objective, validated assessment methods, such as the RMP-MR/DD and the newer RMP-ID, reduce bias in the PCP planning process.

Challenges of PCP

Researchers have identified the following challenges in implementing PCP.

Heller, Factor, Sterns, and Sutton (1996) found that many adults with ID lack some of the skills needed for planning their future.

PCP facilitators often provide consumers with opportunities to make minor decisions (such as what they wear) rather than major ones (such as where they live.)

PCP is a time-consuming, expensive process (Robertson et al., 2007).

Trained facilitators are in short supply, and people are busy and may not attend planning sessions except when paid to so (Robertson et al., 2007).

Even when PCP planning results in the identification of needs, in many instances plans are not implemented (Dumnas, de la Garza, Seay, & Becker, 2002).

PCP is rarely attempted with people with a dual diagnosis (Robertson et al., 2007).

Outcome data are limited.

Reiss Profile of Psychological Needs (RMP-ID)

As was discussed in Chapter 3, the RMP-ID is a standardized assessment of 12 human needs relevant to ID. Although everybody embraces these needs, individuals have different priorities for each need. For the sake of simplicity, the RMP-ID characterizes the strength of a given need in terms of three prioritizations called Green, Red, and Yellow.

> *Green Need* indicates that a given need is stronger-than-average (upper 20% when compared with RMP-ID normative samples). A person with Green Social Contact, for example, needs frequent social experiences to be happy.

> *Red Need* indicates that a given need is weaker-than-average (lower 20% when compared with RMP-ID normative samples). A person with Red Social Contact needs frequent periods of solitude to be happy.

> *Yellow Need* indicates that a given need has average strength (includes 60% of the general population of people with ID.) Yellow needs have minimal implications for PCP.

Person centered planners may ignore Yellow needs because they are usually gratified in the course of everyday life without special scheduling. Planners should attend to the Green (strong) and Red (weak) needs, however, because these are likely to require special lifestyle adjustments to be gratified. Weak/Red needs are just as important for happy lifestyles as are strong/Green needs. Often the difference is only semantic. A weak need for independence, for example, is the same as a strong need for interdependence.

The following comments show the theoretical connections between Green and Red needs and implications for PCP. The system as a whole has been used professionally in counseling and coaching with thousands of people. The model is fully testable scientifically. The order of needs is alphabetical, and these descriptions are backed generally by peer-reviewed scientific studies showing the validity of the RMP and the RMP MR/DD (see Chapter 3). Many specific details, however, are common sense.

Need for Acceptance

This need motivates people to seek approval while avoiding criticism, failure, and rejection. Acceptance is intrinsically valued and is not about something else – it is not about self-love, guilt reduction, or the benefits of favoritism. Acceptance is about wanting others not to criticize you because you simply dislike it.

Satisfaction of this need produces feelings of self-confidence and a can-do attitude, whereas frustration produces feelings of insecurity and fear of failure. People with ID may need acceptance from parents, caregivers in parental roles, and peers. Perhaps the simplest way to know whose acceptance is needed most is to determine whose criticism or loss would hurt the most.

Green Acceptance. People with this need may have considerable difficulty coping with failure, criticism, and/or rejection. They may lack self-confidence and have a tendency to blame themselves when something goes wrong. Some (not all) give inconsistent effort: These individuals hold back effort because failure hurts less when they do not try. Some of the personality traits that may describe them include "insecure," "inconsistent effort," "self-doubting," and for some "indecisive" and/or "pessimistic."

These individuals are happiest when others stand behind them. They react positively to gentle encouragement but negatively to evaluation and explicit or implicit threats of rejection, criticism, and failure.

Planners might discuss how the individual responds to both praise and criticism, the kinds of praise that work best, and the types of criticism that typically produce the most negative reactions. They should also consider how best to encourage the individual to feel more confident, try more things, and have a more positive attitude. Caregivers should not yell at these people and should try to avoid criticism and reprimands. Caregivers might provide a non-evaluative and supportive environment. They might want to be cautious about providing effusive praise or excessive positive reinforcement, however, because such experiences may remind the individual of being evaluated. Experience with each individual should serve as a guide for how much positive reinforcement is best.

Red Acceptance. People with this need usually cope relatively well with failure, criticism, and/or rejection. They may have a "can do" attitude and a potential to learn from constructive feedback. Some of the personality traits that may describe them include "confident," "game" (willing to try things), "optimistic," and "self-assured."

Many people with Red Acceptance have the basic optimism required to go after what they want in life and to expect success. These individuals tend to be happy and usually have a positive, optimistic attitude. They tend to make the most of things. Some (not all) will show consistent effort and have a zest for life.

Planners might wish to discuss the person's most important goals and challenges, as well as how best to ensure that the individual has opportunities to pursue his/her goals.

Need for Attention

This need motivates people to seek notice from others, which is a common way for people with ID to feel respected. In the general population, having status, money, wealth, or social titles are common means of feeling self-important. Attention and respect are intrinsically valued apart from any self-interest they may bring. People feel slighted when they receive less respect/attention than they believe is their due, and they feel flattered when they receive more respect/attention than they believe is their due.

Satisfaction of this need produces feelings of self-importance, whereas frustration produces feelings of insignificance. We attend both to people we respect (generally, those of high status) and to people who are unusual in their appearance or behavior. We tend to ignore people who have low status (deemed to be socially unimportant), people we disrespect, or people who are ordinary in their appearance and their behavior. Since people with ID are not given a high status in many societies, some resort to attention-grabbing behavior or dress to satisfy their need for attention.

Green Attention. People with this need may be strongly motivated to be noticed by other. Some, though not all, may value being "special" and have a tendency to show off, behave dramatically or outrageously, or dress in colorful ways that draw notice. Some (not all) may want to display or own things that are prestigious and, thus, attention grabbing. Some (not all) may seek to hang out with high-status peers. Some (not all) may associate themselves with anything that is popular and dissociate themselves from anything that is unpopular. Some of the personality traits that may describe them include "materialistic," "vain," "show off," "noisy," "dramatic," "unconventional," "formal," and "acts like he/she is special."

Since most people seek to call attention only to those behaviors in which they take pride, individuals differ in what it is about themselves they want others to notice and respect. Some people call attention to their accomplishments, others to their looks or popularity, and still others to prestigious things they own. Since attention is a primal indicator of importance, some (not all) people with Green Attention think negative or unflattering attention indicates a higher degree of status than does being ignored.

Planners might discuss the individual's possible need to feel important or special. The planning groups might consider ways caregivers could make an occasional fuss (e.g., over how the individual is dressed or over something the person did.) Some (not all) people with Green Attention may like to wear colorful clothes. Caregivers might permit the individual to own at least one or two special, attention-grabbing things. They might assign special chores. Some people with Green Attention are materialistic and respond well to special recognitions, such as gold stars or awards. Caregivers should discuss the individual's possible concern with appearance and possible need to dress in "nice" clothes.

These individuals are happiest when they are the center of attention, treated in special ways, or shown respect. They are unhappy when they are ignored.

Planners might consider caregiver attitudes toward the individual's attention-seeking. Do some caregivers mark down this individual because of attention-seeking? What might be done to provide a more respectful and tolerant caregiver attitude? Without permitting the individual to be inappropriate, caregivers should be tolerant of the individual's need for attention.

Red Attention. People with this need may tend to avoid the limelight and may dislike being noticed, given special treatment, or singled out. They may be annoyed by people who demand special treatment. Some (not all) may be conventional in dress and behavior; others may like to dress plainly. Some of the personality traits that may describe them include "quiet," "modest," "humble," "conventional," "plain," and, for some, "egalitarian."

Planners might discuss how caregivers could best respect the individual's wish not to be the center of attention. They might consider an individual's possible need to blend into group or background without being noticed. The individual may prefer clothing selections that do not stand out.

Caregivers may pay such little attention to these individuals they may sometimes forget to take care of their needs. Planners might discuss how best to avoid this possible problem.

Need to Eat

This need motivates people to consume food. As one of the 16 human needs, eating is about satiating one's appetite and experiencing intrinsic pleasures such as good taste; the need for eating does not include eating for health reasons or to gain weight. When we eat because our doctors say we must do so, our eating behavior is not motivated by our appetite and, thus, does not fall under the need to eat.

Satisfaction of this need produces feelings of satiation, whereas frustration produces hunger. Abraham Maslow believed that eating takes primacy over other needs, as in the example of hunger pains interrupting someone who is reading a book. Many people with ID look forward to meals and enjoy eating.

Green Eating. People with this need may have hearty appetites such that food may be among the greatest joys in their lives. They may like to snack and may enjoy many different kinds of food. Not surprisingly, many (not all) may have a tendency to become overweight. Some of the personality traits that may describe them include "gluttonous," "overeater," "voracious," and possibly "hedonistic."

Planners might discuss the individual's preferences for food. What are the person's favorite foods? What can be done to provide an occasional great tasting meal? Some individuals with Green Eating may enjoy cooking or learning to cook.

Planners might discuss the individual's weight. If he/she has a tendency to be overweight, planners might consider the need to avoid obesity by controlling portions. They might consult a nutritionist or, in the case of obesity, a psychologist.

Planners might discuss caregiver attitudes toward the individual's possible overeating. Do some caregivers mark down this individual because of overeating? Do they mistake the individual's intrinsic enjoyment of meals for a lack of self-control? What might be done to provide a more respectful caregiver attitude?

Red Eating. People with this need may have weak appetites. They may rarely snack and may be fussy eaters. Not surprisingly, many (not all) may have a tendency to become underweight. Some of the personality traits that may describe them include "eats like a bird," "eats sparingly," "light eater," and possibly "thin."

Planners might discuss the individual's preferences for food. What are the person's favorite foods? Planners might consider how best to provide a nutritional diet given that the individual may eat less than most people do.

Planners might discuss the individual's weight. If he/she has a tendency to be underweight, they might consult a nutritionist and/or a psychologist.

Need to Help Others

This need motivates altruism – that is, helping others out of kindness rather than self-interest. People with ID can help others by providing assistance to parents or to caregivers when they are nurturing young children; they also can help friends or take care of animals or plants. Helps Others motivates people to provide assistance for no reason other than altruism.

Satisfaction of this need produces feelings of compassion, whereas frustration produces feelings of outrage.

Green Helps Others. People with this need may be happiest when they are doing things for others. The suffering of others may bother them. Some (not all) may enjoy parenting roles or volunteerism and may want to take care of children, the sick, or the downtrodden. They may take pride in their responsible and compassionate nature. Some of the personality traits that may apply to them include "altruistic," "compassionate," "nurturing," "family person," "caring person," "volunteer," "do-gooder," "involved," and "volunteer."

Planners might discuss the individual's need for roles larger than self. What can be done to provide opportunities to take care of a domestic animal or a baby doll?

Planners might discuss the individual's possible need for family. How does he/she react to family gatherings? If the individual enjoys his/her family, what can be done to provide more quality time with family.

Red Helps Others. People with this need may feel burdened when taking care of others in need. They may dislike being a caregiver of any kind, be it for children, animals, or plants. They may dislike parenting roles. They may look the other way when they see others hurt or suffering. Some of the personality traits that may describe them include "hardnosed," "insensitive to suffering of others," "not involved," and possibly "opportunistic" or "expedient."

Planners might discuss the individual's dislike of caregiving and helping others. Does the individual, for example, dislike maternal/ paternal roles? What can be done to respect the individual's preferences in this regard? How might planners ensure that the individual is not encouraged to take care of others?

Planners might discuss the individual's attitude toward his/her family. How does he/she react to family gatherings or visits? If the individual dislikes family gatherings/visit, what might be done to improve the situation?

Need for Independence

This need motivates self-reliance, which is intrinsically valued. People with ID can experience independence by self-determining their own life-styles and activities. Individuals vary, however, in how much support they need when making choices.

Satisfaction of this need produces the joy of personal freedom, where-as frustration produces feelings of dependency.

Green Independence. People with this need may highly value self-reli-ance and may be reluctant to ask for assistance. In order to be happy, they may need to feel they can take care of themselves. Some (not all) will have a need to do things their own way and may be reluctant to go along, to get along. Some (not all) may be leaders rather than followers. Some (not all) may dislike emotional closeness and/or may be so proud they have dif-ficulty expressing gratitude or saying "thank you." Some of the personal-ity traits that may describe them are "independent-minded," "willful," and possibly "stubborn."

Planners might discuss what skills should be taught to help the indi-vidual reach a greater degree of self-reliance. Does he/she react positively or negatively to assistance? Is the individual proud? Does the person like to do his/her own work? Planners also might discuss the ways in which this person expresses his/her individuality.

Red Independence. People with this need may place little value on self-reliance. In order to be happy, these individuals may need to know they can trust others to help them meet their needs. They may seek support, guidance, or assistance. Some (not all) may be followers rather than lead-ers. They may tend to show appreciation when helped. Some (not all) may seek closeness with other people. Some (not all) may be religious or spiritual. Some of the personality traits that may describe them are "interdependent," "nonassertive," "dependent," and possibly "onlooker," "laid-back," and "needy."

Planners might discuss the individual's possible need for emotional support. Does the individual respond positively to assistance? Does the individual respond negatively to being on his/her own without support? Should leadership roles be avoided because they make the individual feel uncomfortable? Is the individual's need to feel supported adequately ad-dressed by current programming, or does more need to be done?

Need for Learning

This need motivates curiosity or learning for its own sake. Although people with ID may be slow learners, they still have the potential to enjoy learning. Satisfaction of this need produces a feeling of wonder, whereas frustration produces boredom or confusion.

Green Learning. People with this need may be life-long learners who enjoy conversation or expressing their ideas. They may show a wide range of interests, ask a lot of questions, and/or enjoy school or formal learning situations. Some of the personality traits that may describe them are "wants to understand things," "talks a lot," and "intellectual."

Planners might discuss the individual's possible need for knowledge. What does the individual want to learn? Does the individual respond better to school learning or to travel/exploring places? Does the individual like to talk a lot, and, if so, how can the planning group encourage caregivers to become good listeners? Is the individual always asking questions, and, if so, how can the planning committee ensure that caregivers are patient and answer questions clearly?

Red Learning. People with this need tend to dislike school learning. They may value practical knowledge they can immediately implement but not abstract ideas or impractical theories. They may have the inclination to learn only a little at a time and may experience annoyance when asked to think or learn at a faster pace. They may become easily frustrated when in school situations. They may ask few questions and may dislike conversations. Some (not all) may dislike people who talk too much. Some of the personality traits that may describe them are "doers," "practical," and "action-oriented."

Planners might discuss the individual's learning style. What is the best pace of learning for this individual? How can the educational curriculum be taught in small, digestible steps? What can be done to increase the practical relevance of the curriculum? How can teachers be encouraged to provide "hands on" learning experiences?

People with Red Curiosity may become annoyed by housemates who talk a lot and ask them many questions. Planners might discuss what can be done to remedy any issues this might cause between the individual and his/her housemates.

Need for Order

This need motivates organizing and cleaning behavior. Order is not about efficiency, but is intrinsically valued apart from any instrumental benefits being organized may bring. People with ID vary considerably in the degree of organization they intrinsically value.

Satisfaction of this need produces feelings of stability and comfort, while frustration produces feelings of chaos and discomfort.

Green Order. People with this need may embrace organized lifestyles, rules, schedules, rituals, sameness, predictability, and cleanliness. They may become upset when routines are not followed or daily schedules are interrupted. They may care about small details. These individuals are happy when they live in a clean, orderly, and stable environment. They are quick to experience discomfort when their clothes, skin, or room become dirty. They may become upset when major changes in their environment occur, such as transfer to another residence. Some (not all) become upset when they are asked to do things on the spot without an opportunity to prepare. Some of the personality traits that may describe them include "organized," "careful," "inflexible," "methodical," "neat," and "tidy."

Planners might discuss the individual's possible needs for routine, order, and stability. They might encourage daily schedules to be followed everyday with minimal changes.

Planners might also discuss the individual's need for cleanliness. How clean and tidy does the individual want his/her residence to be? What could be done to improve the cleanliness of the individual's residence?

Red Order. People with this need may dislike rules, schedules, ritual, sameness, and predictability. They may experience an organized lifestyle as confining. They may be focused on the "big picture" and tend to overlook details. Some (not all) may react with discomfort to immaculately clean and super neat rooms. Some (not all) may be happy when behaving spontaneously, following their nose and doing things on the spur of the moment. They may enjoy variations in daily schedule and have a high tolerance for ambiguity and unpredictability. Some (not all) may have a tendency to try a new task before finishing the last one. Some of the personality traits that may describe them include "flexible," "spontaneous," "changes mind frequently," "sloppy," "disorganized," and perhaps "tardy" and "untidy."

Planners might discuss the individual's preference for spontaneity. What could be done to provide spontaneous experiences? How might caregivers create a moderate degree of variation and flexibility of schedule?

The planners might discuss the individual's possible sloppiness and/or creativity. Do caregivers mark down this individual because of sloppiness? What might be done to provide a more respectful and accepting caregiver attitude? Without permitting the individual to be dirty, caregivers should be tolerant of the individual's tendency to be messy and disorganized.

Need for Physical Activity

This need motivates muscle exercise including vigorous activities. Satisfaction of this need produces the joy of vitality, whereas frustration produces restlessness. People with ID need exercise just like everybody else. Physical activity is intrinsically valued apart from any health benefits it may have.

Green Physical Activity. People with this need may have a zest for exercise and be happiest with an active lifestyle. They may value fitness, vitality, stamina, and possibly strength. Some (not all) may take pride in their athleticism and may become unhappy when inactive for a while. Some of the personality traits that may apply to them are "active," "athletic," "energetic," "fit," "outdoorsy," "perky," and "physical."

Planners should discuss the individual's possible need for physical exercise. What exercises or sports does the individual enjoy most? Is the person athletic? Does the individual enjoy the outdoors? Are current opportunities adequate to exercise and develop physical fitness? Would the individual prefer greater opportunity to play ball, hike, swim, or exercise?

Red Physical Activity. People with this need may dislike exercise and physical exertion. Some (not all) may seek a sedentary lifestyle even when they have no disability limiting physical movements. Some (not all) may be physically lazy or dislike the outdoors. Some (not all) may dislike sports, hiking, swimming, and exercise. They may need encouragement and extrinsic reasons – such as health – to exercise regularly. Some of the personality traits that may describe them include "lackadaisical," "listless," "inactive," and "lethargic."

Planners might discuss the individual's possible need for rest. During athletic games, hikes, etc., do caregivers provide this individual with sufficient opportunities to rest? The planners might also evaluate how fit the individual is. What are the possible long term health implications of the individual's sedentary lifestyle? If the individual is unfit or significantly overweight, the planning committee may discuss possible ways to increase the individual's activity.

Need for Romance

This need motivates sexual activity. Satisfaction of this need produces feelings of ecstasy, whereas frustration produces feelings of lust. The life motive of Romance is moderately correlated with interest in beauty. People with ID have the same sexual needs as everyone else. Romance is intrinsically valued and is not part of a larger motive for sensual pleasure.

Green Romance. People with this need may give significantly above-average priority to sexual experiences. These individuals often may think about sex and may be attracted to many potential partners. Some of the personality traits that may apply to them are "lover," "passionate," "romantic," and perhaps "promiscuous."

Planners might discuss the individual's higher-than-average inter-est in romance. Does the individual have opportunities for relationships? Does he/she have privacy? The planners might discuss caregiver atti-tudes toward the individual's sexuality. Do some caregivers mark down this individual because of sexual behavior? What might be done to provide a more respectful and tolerant caregiver attitude? Without permitting the individual to be inappropriate, caregivers should be tolerant of the indi-vidual's romantic nature.

The planners might consider the individual's possible interest in beau-ty. Is the individual's room and residence physically appealing? Can more be done with decorations? Is the individual interested in art? Does he/she like to draw or paint?

Red Romance. People with this need may give significantly below-av-erage priority to sexual experiences. These individuals may spend little time thinking about and pursuing sex and, while they may occasionally enjoy sex, have little interest in frequent sex. Some (not all) may dislike sex, possibly because they may have doubts about their sexual skills or because they were taught puritanical attitudes and become anxious in sexual situations. Some (not all) may find some aspects of sex disgusting. Some of the personality traits that may apply to them include "celibate," "chaste," "Platonic," and "puritanical." Planners might discuss the indi-vidual's sexuality.

Need for Social Contact

This need motivates interest in social experiences and is closely relat-ed to the need for fun. People with ID need to socialize and have fun just like everybody else. They intrinsically value companionship apart from any other benefits friends might provide. Satisfaction of this motive produces feelings of belonging, whereas frustration produces feelings of loneliness.

Green Social Contact. People with this need may be gregarious. Since they may be happiest when with others, they may value social skills that attract others and keep friends. They may become unhappy when alone for long periods of time. They may enjoy partying and like to have fun. Some of the personality traits that may describe them include "extrovert," "fun-loving," and "friendly."

Dale Carnegie famous book, *How to Win Friends and Influence People* (Carnegie, 1936/1981), advised people to smile, to listen carefully to what the other person has to say, to remember the other person's name and use it often in speech, to avoid criticizing other people, to give deserved praise at every opportunity, and to be concerned with one's appearance. He also advised against being selfish or snobbish.

Planners might discuss the individual's higher-than-average interest in social life, taking into consideration who the individual's friends are, his or her preferred social activities, and any clubs or groups the individual might join if he/she hasn't done so already. They should further discuss how the individual likes to have fun and how caregivers might better support the individual's possible social and fun-loving goals.

Red Social Contact. People with this need may value having a few close friends over having many superficial friends. Some (not all) may show little interest in acquaintances including the people they meet or live with. They may dislike parties and may show little interest in playing with others. Some of the personality traits that may describe them include "private," "serious," "introvert," "loner," and possibly "shy."

Planners might discuss the individual's possible interests in solitude and privacy. How much time is spent alone? Is the individual happy with this situation? Do caregivers understand the individual's need for privacy? The daily schedule might include some group activities, but fewer such activities than most consumers have. The schedule might include time for doing things alone or at least permit the individual to choose between social and private activities.

The planners might discuss caregiver attitudes toward the individual's possible introversion. Do some caregivers mark down this individual because of his/her disinterest in socializing? What can be done to provide a more respectful and tolerant caregiver attitude? Without permitting the individual to live as a hermit, caregivers should be tolerant of the individual's private nature.

Need for Tranquility

This need motivates avoidance of anxiety and pain and, thus, breaks down into correlated components for anxiety sensitivity and pain sensitivity. Satisfaction of this life motive produces relaxation, whereas frustration produces fear, anxiety, or pain.

Green Tranquility. People with this need may give significantly above-average priority to avoidance of anxiety and pain. These individuals may become easily frightened, tend to worry a lot, and exhibit above-average concern for their personal safety. They may have a tendency to handle stress poorly. Some (not all) may have little tolerance for physical pain. Some personality traits that may describe them include "fearful," "anxious," "apprehensive," "cautious," "timid," and possibly "worrier."

Some (not all) people with Green Tranquility may dislike travel or even venturing away from their residence. They may embrace the familiar and avoid the unknown. Some (not all) fear having a panic attack when they are away from their residence.

Planners should discuss level of stress, fears, and sensitivity to pain. What does the individual worry about? What does he/she fear? How could caregivers provide a more worry-free and stress-free life? Is the individual in pain? Is enough being done to manage any stress or pain?

The planners might consider the individual's reactions to travel, especially day trips or vacations. Does the individual react negatively? If so, what types of travel situations arouse the most concerns?

The planners might discuss caregiver attitudes toward the individual's possible nervousness or timidity. Do some caregivers mark down this individual because of a timid nature? What can be done to provide a more respectful and tolerant caregiver attitude? Without permitting the individual to be a coward, caregivers should be tolerant of the individual's risk-aversion.

Red Tranquility. People with this need may exhibit insensitivity to anxiety and pain, at least in comparison with the average person. Some (not all) may seek moderately exciting experiences, possibly embracing dare, travel, risk, and/or adventure. Some of the personality traits that may describe them are "relaxed," "courageous," "adventurers," "fearless," "risk-takers," "worry free," "relaxed," "insensitive to pain," and "venturesome."

Planners might discuss safe ways to increase the excitement in the individual's life. Does the person like adventure? Does he/she enjoy travel? Keeping in mind some level of adventure may be necessary for the person to be happy, the planners might discuss whether or not the individual has a tendency to go to far? If so, what types of training or arrangements might be needed to ensure safety?

Need for Vengeance

This need motivates people to fight back when provoked and to intrinsically value winning. Satisfaction of this life motive produces the thrill of triumph, whereas frustration produces anger.

Green Vengeance. People with this need may confront those who provoke, annoy, or threaten them. Some (not all) may cope poorly with anger, frustration, and/or irritability. Some (not all) may struggle to control their tempers. Some (not all) may hold grudges. Some of the personality traits that may describe them are "competitor," "fighter," "pugnacious," and "combative."

Green Vengeance motivates the competitive spirit. These individuals may be happy in competitive situations and when they win. Some (not all) may enjoy winning so much they become interpersonally competitive. Some (not all) may overreact to losing. Competitive people are quick to confront others, and some (not all) are aggressive. Some (not all) may enjoy confrontation so much they go "looking for trouble." They may admire fighters and disrespect people who back down from confrontation.

Person-centered planners might discuss the individual's possible need for appropriate opportunities for competitive play. They might tolerate a certain degree of combativeness, competitiveness, and flashes of temper or anger and focus on keeping such expressions of emotion from getting out of hand. Some (not all) people with Green Vengeance dislike cooperative play.

Planners might discuss what provokes this individual. If the individual has a significant temper or a problem with aggression, planners might wish to consult with a behavioral psychologist.

Planners might discuss caregiver attitudes toward the individual's competitive spirit. Do some caregivers mark down this individual because of competitive behavior? What might be done to provide a more respectful and tolerant caregiver attitude? Without permitting the individual to be aggressive toward others, caregivers should be tolerant of the individual's competitive nature.

Red Vengeance. People with this need may intrinsically value conflict avoidance, cooperation, and peace-keeping. They may be skilled in reconciliation behaviors and may avoid confrontations, fights, and violence and seek a life that is free of conflict. They may enjoy cooperating with others and may dislike competitive games. Some of the personality traits that may describe them are "cooperative," "kind," "merciful," "non-aggressive," and "peacemaker."

Planners might discuss the individual's possible gentle nature. Does the individual have adequate opportunities for cooperative play? Does he/she have gentle housemates, or is he/she bothered by aggressive housemates? What could be done to lessen the conflict in the individual's life?

Chapter 5

America's Powerless Population

Intellectual disability (ID) and mental health disorders are two different disabilities (Menolascino, 1965). ID is manifested as subaverage intelligence, whereas mental health disorders are indicated by emotional, social, or personality problems. Most people who have ID do not have a mental health disorder, and most people who have a mental health disorder do not have ID. Some people, however, have both disorders, known as "dual diagnosis." I have called them "America's powerless population" because they are underserved with few influential advocates.

People with ID are vulnerable to the full range of mental illnesses. As George Tarjan and Herbet Grossman were fond of saying, "[Intellectual disability] is not an antidote for mental illness." The same mental illnesses seen in the general population are seen in people with ID. (See Chapter 6.)

In the next five chapters of this book, we will consider how human needs play out in dual diagnosis. We begin our discussion with a review of the population of people who have a dual diagnosis.

Consequences of Dual Diagnosis

Mental health disorders have the following unfortunate consequences for people with ID.

1. They may delay personal growth and/or cause significant deterioration in overall adaptive functioning (Schalock & Harper, 1978).

2. They may lead to maladaptive social behaviors that cause failure in employment settings (Greenspan & Shoultz, 1981).

3. They may cause emotional discomfort and pain. Anxiety disorders, for example, may lead to experiences of intense fear and repeated panic attacks. Mood disorders may lead to experiences of despair, hopelessness, and self-hated. Severe behav-

ior disorders may lead to self-injury, self-mutilation, chronic pain, irritability, and overactivity.

4. They may create barriers to residential and educational opportunities in community settings (Bruininks, Hill, & Morreau, 1988; Eyman & Borthwick, 1980; Larson & Lakin, 1992; Schalock & Siperstein, 1996).

Persistence of Dual Diagnosis

Psychiatric symptoms in people with ID sometimes endure for many years with little or no improvement. Reid, Ballinger, Heather, and Melvin (1984) found little change in behavior problems over a 6-year period. James (1986) found little change in the symptoms of affective disorder over time periods of a decade or more. Linden and Forness (1986) found that 70 percent of a sample of 40 people with dual diagnosis still had significant adjustment problems a decade after they began receiving psychiatric treatment. Matson, Coe, Gardner, and Sovner (1991) evaluated 506 residents of four institutions in two states for frequency, severity, and duration of behavior problems. They found that 91.6% of maladaptive behaviors had been evident for at least 12 months. Tonge and Einfeld (2000) found that disruptive behavior, self-absorbed behavior, communications disturbances, anxiety, social relating problems, and antisocial behavior changed little over a four-year period

Psychosocial Risk Factors

Many people with ID are exposed for long periods of time to negative social conditions (Reiss, 1994; Reiss, Levitan, & McNally, 1982). Compared with children with no ID, those with ID are significantly more likely to experience negative life events such as parental separation, parental financial crisis, problem with police, serious illness, and death of a close friend. Specifically, the following negative social conditions are commonly experienced by people with ID.

Peer Rejection. Many children with ID are rejected by their peers and socially isolated in school. As Philips (1967) noted,

> The experience of entering school may present difficulties to the child .... [who] may be more vulnerable in this situation. He may tend to consider himself different and unwanted and set himself apart from others. He may be shunned and teased by his peers, called names and taunted, be the "fall guy" for the class bully and the victim of jokes. Neighbors may forbid

their children to play with him. In reaction ... he may develop a variety of symptoms of emotional disorder (p. 69).

Partially because of peer rejections, public school children with ID are lonelier than their non-ID peers (Luftig, 1988; Williams and Asher, 1982).

Awareness of Stigma. Many people with ID become aware of stigmatizing experiences. They report incidents of being called "retard," of being viewed as incompetent, and of not being asked for their opinions (Reiss & Benson, 1984). A 27 year-old woman with an IQ of 60, for example, complained that her family "treats me like a baby." A 23 year-old man complained that he could not obtain a driver's license or go to college. A 27 year-old man with an IQ of 65 recalled childhood experiences of being ridiculed for riding on the handicapped bus to school. He also expressed significant loneliness related to lack of romantic success. "I'm so lonely," he said, "I can see myself as an old man with gray hairs – no friends, no family, all by myself" (Reiss & Benson, 1984).

Historically, the label "mental retardation" has been associated in the public's mind with "deviance" and "abnormality." Consider, for example, the following remarks by Walter Fernald, who was a pioneer in the field of ID, as cited in Zigler (1971):

"The feebleminded are a parasitic, predatory class, never capable of self-support or of managing their own affairs ... They cause unutterable sorrow at home and are a menace and danger to the community. Feebleminded women are almost invariably immoral ... Every feebleminded person, especially the high-grade imbecile, is a potential criminal, needing only the proper environment and opportunity for the development and expression of his criminal tendencies"

Social Disruption. Children in residential programs may be moved around, disrupting their social networks. Berkson and his colleagues were among the first researchers to document the devastating impact of residential relocations on the loss of friendships (Berkson & Romer, 1980a. b). Reiss (1985) reported the case of an individual who had experienced 19 residential relocations prior to the age of 22. Each relocation meant an abrupt loss of parental figures, peers, and familiar surroundings. At the time of abrupt loss, moreover, the individual was surrounded by strangers and living in an unfamiliar setting. No wonder residential relocations sometimes trigger challenging and protest behaviors.

When children with ID are placed in residential programs outside their home, they often think they were "sent away" because they are unworthy of parental love (Kessler, 1988). Many children may blame themselves for the loss of parents and family.

Baker, Blacher, and Pfeiffer (1993) found that about one-third of the children in residential treatment settings had no family contact. Further, they found that family involvement was less for children with a dual diagnosis than for children with ID who had no mental health disorder.

Segregation. People with ID experience varying degrees of segregation from society, including placement in publicly funded residential facilities. Even people who live at home with their families may have only limited access to community activities because some families control their loved one's access to public events. These families may be trying to protect their loved one from potential dangers, rejection, or stigmatization.

Segregation could have negative impact on the individual's social development, self-concept, and mood. Many researchers have documented the negative effects of segregation including impaired performance on language tasks, learning tasks, and on tasks of emotional understanding (Lustman & Zigler, 1982; Zigler, 1971).

Self-Concept. Many people with ID have a negative view of themselves (Zetlin & Turner, 1984). Widaman, MacMillan, Hemsely, Little, and Balow (1992) found that students with ID have a less positive self-concept as compared with non-ID students. Stephens (1953) suggested that people with ID acquire a sense of being different and tend to experience feelings of inadequacy. Edgerton (1967) observed individuals who tried to hide disability from others and pretended to understand much more than they did. He called this behavior the "cloak of competence."

Restricted Opportunities. People with ID do not have the usual opportunities for a rewarding life. The transition from high school to adult life is particularly difficult (Rusch, DeStefano, Chadsey-Rusch, Phelps, & Szymanski, 1992). Consumers may be left behind when peers start dating, start work, or attend college. For example, many consumers have few opportunities for romance, which reduces their potential social supports and may lead to loneliness. Many consumers will not experience parenthood.

Although some obtain jobs, opportunities for meaningful employment are limited. Many do not have a driver license, which may limit their mobility to places they can walk to. Leisure opportunities also may be limited.

Victimization. Many people with ID have been victims of physical abuse, have been robbed, or were taken advantage of by an employer or older person. Individuals with ID are also more vulnerable to sexual exploitation (Valenti-Hein & Mueser, 1990) and subsequent posttraumatic stress disorder (Ryan, 1993).

Inadequate Social Support. Many consumers have limited access to social support networks, which increases their vulnerability to disorder. The social support network for people with ID consists mostly of family members because many consumers have difficulty finding age-appropriate friends. Kraus, Seltzer, and Goodman (1992) evaluated the social support networks of 418 adults who lived at home. Although the study found wide individual variations in social support, 42.3 percent of the sample had no friends.

Williams and Ashley (1992) evaluated the loneliness of 62 students with mild ID and 62 students with no ID. The results showed that boys with ID were significantly lonelier than were their non-ID peers. No differences, however, were found for girls.

Poor Social Skills. Many people with ID have poor social skill, which reduces their capacity for resolving their life problems (Kopp, Baker, & Brown, 1992). Poor social skills associated with dual diagnosis include difficulty solving everyday social problems (Greenspan & Granfield, 1992; Philips, 1967), poor anger management (Benson, 1990), and inadequate leisure skills.

Social Strain. People with ID may experience significant social strain (Lunsky & Havercamp, 1999) because they have limited freedom to avoid stressful situations or individuals. Social strain (negative forms of social support) may be a factor leading to depression (e.g. Barnett and Gotlib, 1988).

Poor Communication Skills. Carr and Durand (1985a, 1985b) proposed that some people with ID develop severe behavior disorders as a substitute means of communication. As Mundy, Seibert, and Hogan (1985) put it,

> ... communication skills are related to children's ability to effectively interact with others. Thus, it is reasonable to expect that individual differences in communication skills are related to emotional problems in [children with ID] (p.65).

Coping Skills. Although people with ID are exposed to many negative social conditions, only some develop a dual diagnosis. Others manage to cope. Nucci and Reiss (1988) found that some consumers handle frustration reasonably well. In a 2 (Groups) X 3 (Conditions) factorial experiment, people with mild ID and no ID waited to perform a counting task under conditions designed to induce stress, no particular emotional state, or relaxation. Physiological, behavioral, and self-report measures confirmed that the Stress Condition actually induced stress. The results showed that stress led to similar improvements in task performance for both groups of participants – those with mild and no ID. The authors concluded the following:

> The idea that [people with ID] readily fall apart when frustrated or stressed might be an invalid, stereotypic conception. Although some [people with ID] might have great difficulty handling stress, others might be able to cope very well, so that overall there is little or no association between intelligence and the capacity to handle stress. In this regard, [Nucci] observed an incident in which a [woman with ID] fell down while leaving the experiment. The woman bruised herself and was in obvious pain. Nevertheless, she kept her wits about her, remained calm during the ride to university hospital, and was able to respond effectively to the physicians' questions about the incident ... The woman handled the stress of the accident quite well, contradicting stereotypic notions that people with ID readily fall apart under conditions of stress" (p. 166).

Prevalence

Between 30% and 40% of individuals with ID are in need of mental health services (Nezu, Nezu, & Gill-Weiss, 1992; Reiss, 1994). Given a prevalence rate of ID at about one percent of the general population - or about 3 million people in the United States – it can be estimated that about one million Americans have a dual diagnosis. This estimate reflects only the one-day prevalence rate (the rate of dual diagnosis on any given day.) The lifetime prevalence rate, which has not been determined, is likely much greater.

Reiss (1990) reported the prevalence of psychiatric symptoms in a randomly selected sample of consumers served by Chicago metropolitan community agencies. Social inadequacy was the most common symptom, reported to be a problem or a major problem for 45.4 percent of the sample. Personality symptoms (e.g., attention-seeking, dependent, nonassertive) were reported for 39.8 percent of the sample; aggression for 25.5 percent; anxiety for 20.6 percent; sadness for 17.7 percent; and psychotic symptoms for 5.8 percent of the sample. Drug abuse, sexual problems, and suicide each were reported to be a problem for 2.0 percent of the sample.

Reiss (1994) suggested that the greater prevalence of psychiatric disorders for people with ID is largely attributable to the higher prevalence of personality disorders and aggressive behavior. Mental illnesses – anxiety disorder, mood disorder, psychosis – are about as prevalent in the ID population as in the general population.

Tonge and Einfeld (2000) studied a representative sample of 582 consumers aged 4-19 at the time of initial evaluation and again four years later. About 40 percent of the sample had psychiatric symptoms – such as disruptive behavior, anxiety, and antisocial behavior -- that persisted for at least four years.

Lakin, Doljanic, Taub, Giuseppina, and Byun (2007) reported data on 2,720 people receiving Medicaid Home and Community-Based Services and Intermediate Care Facility services. Nearly one-third of the sample (31.4 percent) had psychiatric disorders. These individuals with dual diagnosis were found in more restrictive residential programs than was suggested by the severity of ID alone. They were much more likely to receive medications for mood, anxiety, and/or behavior disorders compared with those with ID alone.

Cooper, Smiley, Morrison, Williamson, and Allan (2007) surveyed 1,023 adolescents and adults aged 16 and over living in greater Glasgow, Scotland. The case ascertainment methods, although believed to be comprehensive, yielded twice as many people with moderate/profound ID severity than with mild ID severity. Since mild ID is much more common than moderate/profound, the Cooper et al. results may undercount this group. Six nurses screened the entire sample and referred those suspected of mental illness to one of the project's psychiatrists, who were made aware of the reason for referral before undertaking clinical exams. The results indicated a point prevalence of dual diagnosis of 40.9 percent based on clinical diagnosis (rates also varied significantly lower when different mental illness classification systems were used) and included mental, behavioral, and personality disorders. For mental disorders – psychotic, affective, and anxiety – Cooper at al. reported a rate of 14.8 percent. These results were similar to those obtained with other surveys of large population registries (Lakin et al., 2007) as well as those obtained with a randomly chosen sample (Reiss, 1990).

Studies Comparing People with and without ID. A number of studies have directly compared the rates of mental health disorders for individuals with and without ID. The best known of these studies was a survey of the entire population of children ages 9, 10, and 11 living on the Isle of Wight in the United Kingdom (Rutter, Tizard, Graham & Whitmore, 1970). The estimated prevalence rate for mental health disorders among children with ID was 30% based on parent interviews and 42% based on teacher ratings. These numbers compared with an overall rate of only 7% prevalence for mental health disorders for the general population. Thus, the Isle of Wight studies found that prevalence rates of mental health disorders were five to seven times higher for children with ID as compared to those without ID.

Cullinan, Epstein, and Olinger (1983) compared ratings on the Revised Behavior Problem Checklist for 146 females with mild ID and for 227 females without ID, all of whom were between the ages of 7 and 18.9 years. The group with mild ID scored higher for the occurrence of conduct problems, personality disorders, social inadequacy, and social delinquency. In a followup study, Epstein, Cullinan, and Polloway (1986) compared the ratings for 360 students with educable ID and 360 students with no ID. The students with ID had significantly higher scores for aggression, attention deficit disorder, anxiety-inferiority, and social incompetence.

Koller, Richardson, Katz, and McLaren (1983) evaluated 221 young adult consumers for emotional problems, hyperactive behavior, aggressive behavior, and antisocial behavior. Compared with matched peer controls, people with ID were found to be two and one half times more likely to have a mental health disorder and seven times more likely to have a severe behavior disorder.

In a survey of the records of the Canadian army, Dewan (1948) studied 2,055 men with ID and 28,192 without ID. The age range was 18 to 40 (average 25). An IQ score was estimated from the army M test; psychiatrists who had access to the men's historical data, including previous medical and psychiatric records, interviewed the recruits and rated their emotional stability. Dewan (1948) found that psychiatrists rated 47.7% of men with ID as emotionally unstable, versus 19.7% of men without ID. Thus the prevalence of "emotional instability" was twice as great in men with ID compared with their control peers.

Residential Settings. A large body of data indicates that mental health disorders increase referral to residential institutions and create barriers to community and social integration (Bruininks, Hill, Morreau, 1988; Eyman & Borthwick, 1980). For these reasons, the rate of mental health disorders is very high in state-operated, institutional settings.

Lakin, Hill, Hauber, Bruninks, and Heal (1983) conducted a series of comprehensive studies on the prevalence of severe behavior disorders in various residential settings. The research, which was national in scope, analyzed behavior disorders in terms of categories of "injures self,' "injures other people," and "destructive to property" (Bruininks, Hill, Weatherman, & Woodcock, 1986). They found very high rates of severe behavior disorders in large state-operated institutions. Only three states had rates of less than 30%, whereas 20 states had rates of 50% or more.

Although most studies have found lower rates of mental health disorders in community settings versus large state institutions, the rates in the community are still significant. Bruininks and his colleagues found that rates for "injures self" varied from 10% within semi-independent living environments to 31% for group homes. The rates for behavior that is hurtful to others varied from 14.1% in semi-independent living settings to 35.6% in group homes. The rates for family and foster care living arrangements were between those for semi-independent living and large institutions.

Age. Mental health disorders have been demonstrated across the life span (Borthwick-Duffy, 1994). The results of a number of large surveys showed lower rates for children versus adults (Rojahn, Borthwick-Duffy, & Jacobson, 1993). In a study of 583 children and adolescents, moreover, Reiss and Valenit-Hein (1994) found that mean symptom scores were significantly lower for children under the age of 11 versus adolescents 11-21.

ID Severity. No consistent results have been reported for prevalence as a function of ID severity. Some large-scale surveys have reported higher rates of mental health disorders for persons with mild versus severe ID (Borthwick-Duffy, 1994; Jacobson, 1982a, b), but others have reported lower rates for persons with mild versus severe ID (e.g., Koller, Richardson, Katz, McLaren., 1983; Lund, 1985; Philips & Williams, 1975).

Diagnostic Overshadowing

For 87 days, Mark Wheatley has been locked in a psychiatric ward at Johns Hopkins Hospital. The Baltimore man was ready to leave two months ago, but no person, no agency would take him: In addition to having a psychiatric problem he is also mentally retarded.

While waiting for a home, Wheatley, 29, endured the taunts of other patients, who were troubled mentally but of normal intelligence. He was restrained and shut in seclusion. He had to watch everyone else go home (Sugg, 19991, p. 1a).

As in the example of Mark Wheatley, people who have dual diagnosis constitute one of the most underserved populations in the United States (Reiss, Levitan, & McNally, 1982). Paradoxically, ID increases the risk of mental health disorders and decreases the opportunity for community-based mental health services. The vast majority of people with a dual diagnosis are unable to advocate for themselves, and few advocates or organizations have prioritized their needs. In medical schools, dual diagnosis usually falls through a crack between pediatrics and psychiatry, so that few physicians are trained to provide appropriate medical supports to this population. In the community, individuals with a dual diagnosis may be referred back and forth between mental health and developmental disabilities programs.

Part of the problem is that psychiatric disorders have been underdiagnosed in people with ID, partially because we attribute their inappropriate behavior to their ID rather than to a distinct mental illness. Reiss, Levitan, & Szyszko (1982) introduced the term *diagnostic overshadowing* to refer to instances in which the presence of ID decreases the diagnostic significance of accompanying emotional and behavioral disorders. Just as a six-inch line appears smaller than it really is when viewed next to a ten-inch line, the debilitating effects of mental health disorders appear less significant than they really are when viewed in the context of the debilitating effects of ID.

In the first experimental study on diagnostic overshadowing, a case description of a debilitating fear was presented to three groups of psychologists. The case described a young man who had commuted to and from work at a fast food restaurant for more than a year. One day the man took the wrong bus home, was robbed, and subsequently stopped riding the bus and lost his job. The psychologists were asked to rate the suggested fear on a number of psychological scales and to provide diagnostic impressions and recommendations for interventions.

The three groups differed only in terms of the information that was added to the basic case description. One group rated the fear of an individual who was suggested to have ID; a second group rated the fear for an individual who was suggested to have alcoholism; and a third group rated the fear for an individual who was suggested to have average intelligence.

The results indicated that the same debilitating fear was less likely to be considered an example of an anxiety disorder when the individual was suggested to have ID as compared to average intelligence. In other words, the presence of ID overshadowed the diagnostic significance of the evidence of a debilitating fear (avoidance of commuting, causing loss of job). Additionally, the psychologists were significantly less likely to recommend the appropriate therapy (desensitization) for people with ID. Diagnostic overshadowing also occurred for the alcoholism condition.

The results of subsequent experiments extended diagnostic overshadowing to cases involving schizophrenia and personality disorder (Reiss, Levitan, & Szyszko, 1982). The amount of previous clinical experience with people with ID was unrelated to overshadowing (Reiss & Szyszko, 1983). The phenomenon was demonstrated with both social workers and with psychologists (Levitan & Reiss, 1983).

Goldsmith and Schloss (1984) extended diagnostic overshadowing to learning disabilities and hearing impairment. They used a hypothetical case of a 17-year old female who accidentally rode the wrong bus and ended up in an alley where she was accosted by a man. Subsequently, the woman refused to take any public transportation and lost her job. The school psychologists' were less likely to diagnose a mental health disorder when the case summary included a primary diagnosis of hearing impairment or learning disability versus no primary diagnosis. The school psychologists were also less likely to recommend appropriate services for students with a learning disability or hearing impairment.

Mason and Scior (2004) demonstrated diagnostic overshadowing for case vignettes rated by 133 psychologists and 90 psychiatrists. Sprengler, Strohmer, and Prout (1990) reported evidence of diagnostic overshadowing when ratings were made for hypothetical consumers at IQ 58 but not at IQ 70 or 80. These researchers found that overshadowing was unrelated to professional experience defined as the number of different individuals assessed, but that the tendency for diagnostic overshadowing declined with increasing number of years in the field of ID.

The potential impact of diagnostic overshadowing on mental health services was summarized by Reiss and Szyszko as follows:

> Service delivery typically requires interdisciplinary staffing, leading to a diagnosis of [a mental health disorder] and a recommendation for treatment, a case manager who acts on the recommendation, state administrators who recognize the [mental health aspects] of mental retardation to be sufficiently important to fund appropriate services, and community clinics capable of providing the relevant services. If overshadowing is interpreted as a tendency to view the [mental health disorders of people with ID] as less important than they really are, the phenomenon can influence the delivery of services at any of a variety of points in the case management process. For example, even in instances in which diagnosis and treatment recommendations are made, the service might not be delivered if the case manager assumes that the recommendation for psychotherapy is less important than the recommendation for other services. (1983, p. 401)

Jopp and Keys (2001) reviewed the evidence for diagnostic overshadowing and concluded that the experimental phenomenon is robust. They also found a need for research aimed at evaluating the practical implications suggested by Reiss and Szyszko (1983). Mason and Scio (2004) also concluded that more research is needed to determine the extent of practical implications, which they thought likely but concluded was unproved.

Conclusion

People with ID are vulnerable to the same mental health disorders as is everybody else. These disorders include both mental illnesses (DSM Axis I disorders) that have sudden onsets as well as personality and severe behavior disorders (DSM Axis II disorders) that manifest gradually during adolescence and young adulthood.

Mental health disorders can have more severely negative consequences for people with ID versus those with no ID. These include delayed personal growth, unemployment, emotional pain and suffering, and restricted access to the community including placement in residential agencies. Because people with ID generally have poor problem solving and communication skills, mental health disorders tend to last a long time, perhaps years or decades.

Compared with their no ID counterparts, people with ID have greater exposure to negative social conditions believed to cause or contribute to the occurrence of mental health disorders. These include peer rejection, stigmatization, residential relocation, segregation, and social strain.

Personality disorders and behavior problems, so-called DSM Axis II conditions, are much more prevalent for people with ID versus the general population. Some estimates suggest that as many as one third of adolescents and adults with ID have a DSM Axis II disorder. In contrast, ID prevalence rates for DSM Axis I mental illnesses are about the same as in the general population or perhaps moderately higher, but they are not two or three times higher as is the case with Axis II disorders.

Although mental health disorders occur more frequently, last longer, and have more severe consequences for people with ID versus those with no ID, people with a dual diagnosis are underserved. Because of diagnostic overshadowing, the mental health disorders of people with a dual diagnosis are seen as less significant than they really are, perhaps because people invalidly attribute the maladaptive behavior of this population to ID versus a co-occurring mental illness. People with a dual diagnosis are powerless because they lack understanding and influential advocates. Paradoxically, ID increases the odds of a mental health disorder while decreasing the opportunity for appropriate treatment for such disorders.

Chapter 6

Mental Illness and Intellectual Disabilities

The "dual diagnosis" movement represented a significant broadening of psychiatric interests in the ID field. Before dual diagnosis advocacy, clinicians were focused on the treatment of severe behavior disorders such as aggression, stereotypy, and self-injurious behavior. Dual diagnosis researchers have shown that people with ID are vulnerable to the full range of mental health disorders including mood disorders, anxiety disorders, psychosis, substance abuse, and sexual disorders.

Anxiety Disorders

Anxiety is a normal emotional reaction to danger. This emotion is manifested by nervousness, arousal, stress, and worry. The common signs of anxiety are as follows:

> Autonomic arousal, indicated by rapid heart rate, rapid breathing, sweating, muscle tension, dry mouth, and nausea;

> Behavior such as avoidance, pacing, and shaking;

> Cognitions of apprehension, impending harm, and impending danger.

Both the autonomic and behavior symptoms of anxiety are readily observable in people with ID, but the cognitive signs cannot be established for consumers who are nonverbal.

Anxiety Disorders are severe disruptions in everyday functioning caused by intense or prolonged anxiety and/or avoidance behavior. Some subtypes are as follows:
- Panic Disorder (with/without Agoraphobia)
- Specific Phobia
- Social Phobia
- Obsessive-Compulsive Disorder
- Posttraumatic Stress Disorder

There is conflicting evidence concerning the rate of anxiety disorders in persons with ID. Low rates were reported by Jacobson (1990) in a New York State registry of 42,479 persons with ID, as well as in surveys of outpatient dual diagnosis clinics by both Reiss and Trenn (1984) and Eaton and Menolascino (1982). On the other hand, rates comparable or higher than those for the general population were reported by Craft (1959), Benson (1985), and Reid (1980). Bouras and Drummond (1992) reported a 6.6 percent rate for anxiety disorders among a large sample referred for psychiatric evaluation. Epstein, Cullinan, and Polloway (1986), who asked teachers to rate 360 students with ID and 360 students without ID on the Behavior Problem Checklist, obtained ratings for anxiety that were significantly higher for the students with ID. Further, Knights (1963) found greater anxiety and defensiveness for 128 children with ID than for 178 children with no ID.

Panic Disorder. Panic attacks are indicated by shortness of breath, dizziness, palpations, trembling, sweating, choking, abdominal distress, depersonalization, numbness, hot flashes, chest discomfort, fear of dying, and fear of going crazy or doing something uncontrolled. McNally (1991) has suggested that panic attacks may be rare for persons with ID, especially those with severe/profound ID, because these individuals lack the cognitions associated with such attacks. (See discussion on anxiety sensitivity in Chapter 8.)

Specific and Social Phobias. Phobic anxiety is sometimes expressed in people with ID by crying, tantrums, freezing, or clinging (Fletcher, Loschen, Stavrakaki, & First, 2007a, b). Specific phobias are excessive and persistent fears of particular stimuli, such as snakes or thunderstorms. Social phobias are excessive and persistent fears of being embarrassed or humiliated, such as phobias for public speaking or going to parties. In all phobias, a consumer invariably experiences intense fear if the phobic situation is encountered. As a result, the social phobic is motivated to go to great lengths to avoid social encounters, but some social phobics with ID might not be able to do this because of a severe absence of choice (Fletcher, Loschen, Stavrakaki, & First, 2007a, b).

Matson (1981a) reported three cases of long-standing social avoidance in girls with ID aged 8 to 10 years. The children's fears, which had been evident for six months prior to referral for treatment, limited their ability to function at home and at school.

Persons with ID can acquire fear to a wide range of stimuli. Researchers have reported case histories of test anxiety (Knights, 1963), bus phobia (Obler & Terwilliger, 1970), social anxiety (Chiodo & Maddux, 1985), fear of heights (Guralnick, 1973), and fear of community activities (Matson, 1981). One study found four primary themes: fears of separation, natural events, injury, and animals (Guarnaccia & Weiss, 1974). Fear is more common among children than adults (Knapp, Barrett, Groden, & Groden, 1992), but adults with ID have fears that that appear to be similar to those of children matched for mental age (Duff, LaRocca, Lizzet, Martin, Pearce, et al., 1981).

Obsessive Compulsive Disorder (OCD). Obsessions are recurrent, intrusive, anxiety-based thoughts, images, or impulses that often pertain to contamination (e.g., "I might get a disease by touching the doorknob") or to worry (e.g., "Did I turn off the oven"). Compulsions are repetitive behaviors and thoughts designed to reduce or to prevent anxiety, objective disasters, or both. True compulsions do not produce pleasure but may provide temporary relief from anxiety. (Consequently, frequent gambling or drinking are not considered examples of OCD.)

OCD in the general population is associated with above average intelligence (Rasmussen & Tsuang, 1984). Thus, we should expect to find relatively low rates of obsessions and compulsions for people with ID (McNally & Ascher, 1987; Novosel, 1984).

Even so, OCD has been reported for people with ID. Vitiello, Spreat, and Behard (1989) surveyed 283 residents of the Woodhaven residential facility and found that ten (3.5%) could be diagnosed as having OCD. Matson (1982) reported three men with mild ID whose excessive concerns with personal cleanliness were associated with repeatedly checking their clothes, which interfered with their performance at a sheltered workshop. McNally and Calamari (1989) reported a case study of a 51 year-old single, white woman with an IQ of 54 who lived in a group home and had obsessions about contaminations from other people. When an interviewer extended his hand to shake hers, she became visibly anxious, withdrew, and cried out that he was dirty. She became increasingly anxious during the interview and eventually ran to the bathroom to wash her hands. Her OCD prevented her from making friends and interfered with her productivity at work.

Diagnosing OCD in the ID population is complicated when the individual cannot report the unwanted nature of ritual, compulsion, or obsession. Researchers have yet to determine, for example, whether or not stereotypic behavior is OCD. If such behaviors are motivated by anxiety reduction, they would indeed be symptoms of OCD; but if they are motivated by pleasure or other non-anxiety causes, they would not be symptoms of OCD.

Posttraumatic Stress Disorder (PTSD). Some individuals exposed to traumatic events outside the range of ordinary experience develop symptoms of PTSD. These symptoms include a persistent tendency to re-experience traumatic events in flashbacks, recollection, play (in children), and dreams. The person shows a persistent avoidance of stimuli and symbols associated with the trauma.

By definition, PTSD is a reaction to a trauma. Originally, "trauma" referred to extraordinary events that posed a threat of death or serious injury, such as combat, rape, or earthquake (McNally, 2003). Today, the definition of "trauma" is much broader and is sometimes interpreted as almost anything that causes significant stress or horror, such as being the butt of jokes at work. As a result of this conceptual "bracket creep," PTSD is diagnosed much more often today. For people with ID, some authorities interpret trauma to include "developmental milestones, resident placement, and even consensual sexual experiences" (Fletcher, Loschen, Stavrakaki, & First, 2007a, b).

PTSD has been reported for people with ID. Heller (1982) reported PTSD-like behavior in some persons who experienced involuntary residential relocations. Ryan (1994) presented 51 cases of PTSD in persons with ID. The most frequent traumas in Ryan's work were sexual abuse, physical abuse, and life-threatening neglect.

In a study of 105 male Vietnam combat veterans, McNally and Shin (1994) reported that PTSD symptom severity increased as intelligence and education decreased. The results provided initial evidence that subaverage intelligence may be a risk factor for severe PTSD symptoms in people exposed to trauma. The relevance of these results for ID, however, have yet to be investigated.

Mood Disorders

These disorders are indicated by abnormal occurrences of "high" (elated) and/or "low" (depressed) mood states. The "high" mood states are called *mania*, and the "low" mood states are called *depression*. In many cases of depression, excessive or inappropriate anger is present. Mood disorders also are called "affective disorders." To meet the criteria for a mood disorder, an individual must present with a disturbance in mood as the dominant feature. The diagnostician, moreover, needs to rule out various medical causes of mood disturbance, such as possible seizure disorders (Fletcher et al., 2007a, b).

Prior to the 1975, many psychologists mistakenly thought that people with ID lacked the cognitive capabilities needed to become depressed (Gardner, 1967). Subsequently, clinical researchers published a number of case studies to document the occurrence of depression in people with ID (Matson, 1982; Reid, 1976; Reiss & Trenn, 1984; Russell & Tanguay, 1981; Symanski & Biderman, 1984). Further, Sovner and Hurley (1983) published a scholarly review that helped establish the fact that people with ID are vulnerable to mood disorders.

Major Depression. This diagnosis is made only when symptoms last two weeks or longer. The chief symptom is sadness/melancholia. Other symptoms are low energy/fatigue; eating problems (either poor appetite or overeating); and changes in usual sleep patterns (e.g., difficulty falling asleep, difficulty staying asleep, or oversleeping). Negative thinking is pervasive: Depressed people have a negative view of themselves ("I am worthless"), the future ("things will never get better"), and the environment ("the world stinks"; "everything is rotten"). In depression, self-esteem may be so low the individual endorses extreme statements such as, "I am ugly," "I am incompetent," "I am worthless," and even, "I am so worthless, I don't deserve to live."

Depressed people tend to lose interest in formerly enjoyable activities. Little or nothing interests them anymore – for example, they may not want to go anywhere nor do anything. Many depressed people are so preoccupied with their own misery they show little interest in others.

The cognitive signs of depression – such as hopelessness and negative thinking – can be difficult to assess in nonverbal persons with IQs below 50. When diagnosing these individuals, a number of experts have suggested focusing on the behavioral and vegetative signs of depression (Sovner, 1986; Szymanski & Biderman, 1984).

Reiss (1988) provided psychometric support for diagnosing depression in persons with ID. On the "Reiss Screen for Maladaptive Behavior" rating tool, the psychometric scale Depression (P) evaluated physical symptoms such as eating problems, sleep problems, and low energy, whereas the psychometric scale Depression (B) evaluated behavioral symptoms such as sadness, anxiety, irritability, and crying spells. Depression (P) is well suited for assessing the non-cognitive symptoms of depression.

Charlot, Doucette, and Mezzacappa (1993) evaluated two groups of 30 residents of a large state facility. One group had been diagnosed as having affective disorder, and the other group had various mental health disorders other than affective disorder. The investigators interviewed staff members and discovered that the Affective Disorders Group was significantly more likely to have poor appetite, fatigue, withdrawal, and episodic behavior.

Reid (1972a, 1972b) reported cases of affective disorder with psychotic symptoms in people with ID. Some of the people did not complain of feeling depressed and some had attempted suicide.

Szymanski and Biederman (1984) reported case studies of depression in persons with Down syndrome, including a case of anorexia nervosa in

STEVEN REISS

which there was extreme weight loss caused by a refusal to eat. These authors cited an unpublished report from Szymanki and Doherty of six cases of affective disorder in people with mild/moderate ID and nine cases of affective disorder in people with severe /profound ID.

Laman (1989) studied the mood of 36 adults with ID over periods varying between 14 and 30 months (average 21.9 months). The participants had been selected from either sheltered workshops or a developmental disabilities mental health clinic. The results showed a .4 correlation between depressed mood at Time-1 and depressed mood at Time-2. The statistically significant correlation was obtained despite the introduction of antidepressant medication therapy between Time-1 and Time-2. The findings showed that for some consumers depressed mood can persist for at least 30 months.

Depressed mood is sometimes associated with aggressive behavior or anger (e.g., Dosen & Gielen, 1993; Reiss & Rojahn, 1993). In the protest-despair reaction to loss, anger and irritability give way to depressed mood (Suomi, Eiselle, Grady, & Harlow, 1975). Further, some psychoanalysts have described depression as anger turned against the self (Abraham, 1911).

Reiss and Rojahn (1993) evaluated the association between aggression and depression in 528 adults, adolescents, and children with ID. The participants had been rated on either the adult or child versions of the Reiss screening instruments. Criterion levels of aggression were found in 40.4 percent of the depressed participants, but in only 9.9 percent of the nondepressed participants. For both children and adults, the presence of depression was associated with a fourfold increase in criterion levels of conduct problems and aggressive behavior. Using statistical analyses, moreover, Reiss and Rojahn (1993) obtained evidence that anger mediates the association between aggression and depression. In a study of 798 consumers in Germany, Meins (1993) found that scores on a modified German-language Children's Depression Inventory (CDI; Kovacs, 1985) were correlated -.33 with "behavior problems."

Benson and Ivins (1992) investigated the relationship among anger, self-concept, and depression for a sample of 130 adults with mild-moderate ID and found that depression was related to low self-esteem but not to anger. The results regarding anger were inconsistent with those reported by other investigators.

Schloss (1982) observed nine depressed and nine nondepressed adult residents of a large ID facility. Both staff and peers were less likely to approach the depressed people when there was no specific purpose to the interaction, presumably because it is usually unpleasant to interact with someone who is depressed. Schloss' (1982) findings suggest that de-pressed many consumers may be lonely and socially isolated.

Reiss and colleagues evaluated the psychosocial correlates of de-pressed mood in 28 adults with dual diagnosis and 17 mentally healthy adults with ID (Reiss & Benson, 1985; Benson, Reiss, Smith, & Laman, 1985). All of the participants had IQs above 55. The study found that de-pressed mood was significantly correlated both with low levels of social support and with poor social skills. Low levels of social support were as-sociated more strongly with depression than with psychopathology gener-ally.

Laman and Reiss (1987) identified specific social skill deficits associ-ated with depressed mood. The participants were 45 adults with mild ID recruited from either a sheltered workshop or a developmental disabilities mental health outpatient clinic. Compared with the nondepressed people, the depressed people were rated as preoccupied, withdrawn, insecure, an-gry, and antisocial.

In a follow-up study, Laman (1989) reevaluated 36 participants 14 to 30 months after initial assessment. Using path analysis statistics, Laman demonstrated that depression, poor social skills, and low levels of social support were stable over time periods of up to 30 months. The hypothesis that best explained the correlations over time was that poor social skills are risk factors for both low levels of social support and depressed mood. Theoretically, poor social skills could lead to low levels of social support, and loneliness could lead to depressed mood.

Meins (1993) found low levels of social support in a group of 38 adult consumers with a depressive disorder. After a series of multiple regres-sion analyses, Meins (1993) concluded that, "low social support is specific to depression and not characteristic of behavior problems in general" (p. 152).

Bipolar Disorder. This disorder is indicated by episodes of mania, whose chief symptoms include sudden bursts of euphoria and excessive activity. Other symptoms are excessive optimism, overly confident to the point of grandiosity, decreased need for sleep, overly talkative, racing thoughts (flight of ideas), irritability, excessive seeking of pleasurable ac-tivities, and distractibility.

A bipolar person's mood may swing between manic and depressive phases or between manic and normal phases. Reid and Naylor (1976) described cases with short or rapid cycling bipolar disorder. The phrase "rapid cycling" indicates as least four manic episodes within the last 12 months.

A number of authors have discussed the difficulties of diagnosing bipolar disorder in persons with severe ID, who cannot self-report their mood (Berney & Jones, 1988; Reid & Naylor, 1976). It has been suggested that in such cases diagnoses should focus on genetic history, irritability, changes in activity levels, changes in sleep patterns, and the loss of developmental skills such as continence. Einfeld and Wurth (1989) suggested that facial appearance, interest in activities, social responsiveness, somatic complaints, the cognitive content of play, and the full range of the vegetative symptoms of depression should be taken into account.

Suicide

A number of case studies of suicidal behavior in people with ID have been published (e.g., Menolascino, Lazer, & Stark, 1989: Sternlicht, Pustel, Deutsch, 1970). Reiss (1990) found that three of 205 randomly selected people were rated as having a "problem" with suicidal tendencies and that one additional person was rated as having a "major problem."

Benson and Laman (1988) compared 22 suicide attempters with 22 nonsuicidal individuals, all 44 of whom were outpatients at a dual diagnosis clinic. In this study the IQ range was 60 to 80. There were few differences between the two groups in terms of demographic variables except that women were overrepresented in the suicide group. The suicide group had greater problems with anger and depression and half of them made more than one attempt. The most common precipitating factors were problems at school, work, or with a boyfriend/girlfriend.

Lunsky (2004) conducted structured interviews with 98 adults with mild and borderline ID suspected of possible depression. About one-third of the participants had suicidal ideation, such as thinking that life is not worth living. Suicidal ideation was associated with loneliness, stress, anxiety, depression, and low levels of social support.

Schizophrenia

In schizophrenia, behavior is out of sync with reality. Hearing voices is normal when somebody is speaking but not when nobody is there; smiling is normal when one is happy but not when one is angry.

The chief symptoms of schizophrenia are delusions (firmly held false beliefs) and hallucinations (false sensory perceptions, especially hearing voices). Regression (deterioration in adaptive behavior often manifested by poor personal hygiene) is common. The most common hallucinations are auditory (hearing voices); other symptoms may include any combination of the following:

> Cognitive symptoms, such as disorganized speech/ incoherence and memory abnormalities.

Communication symptoms, such as bizarre speech, made-up words, word salad, and redundant speech.

Motor abnormalities, such as catatonic nonresponsiveness, immobility, aimlessness, and bizarre postures.

Affective symptoms, such as flat/blunted affect (rarely smiling), inappropriate affect (e.g., giggling/ smiling over painful experiences or intense anger).

Social symptoms, such as withdrawal, poor social skills, bizarre behavior, or paranoia (extreme suspiousness).

History. In the mid 1800s, the French physician Morel maintained that insanity and ID were both caused by a "tainted heredity" (Zilboorg & Henry, 1941). He constructed detailed tables of the diagnostic signs of various hereditary weaknesses, including the "degenerative trait" in which tainted heredity became progressively more debilitating with each successive generation. The theory of a degenerative trait held that ID and psychosis are two variations of the same disease process. Modern scientific studies have shown that the theory of a degenerative trait is invalid.

In 1888 Hurd distinguished between ID and insanity. He held that insanity could be recognized in people with mild ID but not in people with severe ID.

In the early 1900s Kraepelin suggested that autism was a special type of psychosis called "pfropfschizophrenie." He later abandoned this viewpoint and instead distinguished autism from schizophrenia.

Severity of ID. Adolescents and adults with mild ID are capable of self-reporting hallucinations and delusions, but they sometimes report unimaginative or simplistic fantasies easily mistaken for delusions and hallucinations. Szymanski (1980), for example, reported the case study of a lonely boy who invented an imaginary friend. The boy knew the friend was imaginary, and he showed no other features of schizophrenia. Szymanski concluded that the imaginary friend was not a hallucination.

Since psychiatrists rely on self-reports to identify hallucinations and delusions, some psychiatrists have suggested that schizophrenia cannot be diagnosed in nonverbal people who have IQs below about 50 (Herskovitz & Plesset, 1941; Reid, 1972b, 1993). In advancing this position, Reid (1993) cited Batchelor (1964):

The diagnosis of schizophrenia is clinical and based on various symptoms which tend to be language-based. The significance of these symptoms has to be evaluated against the background of previous personality, the mode of onset of disability, and the course of the illness. The main symptoms include ideas of influence, made experiences, auditory hallucinations, thought disorder, primary delusions, and abnormalities of affect and motility.

Reid's position – that schizophrenia is difficult, if not impossible, to diagnose for nonverbal individuals with IQs under 50 -- has been embraced by the Royal College of Physicians. The authors of NADD's classification manual also embraced this position (Fletcher et al., 2007a, b).

The alternative viewpoint is that psychosis can be diagnosed in persons with IQs below 50 based on psychiatric symptoms other than hallucinations and delusions. These symptoms include regression, withdrawal, emotional blunting, inappropriate affect, poor social skills, and inattention. Perhaps biological markers will be discovered someday to facilitate diagnosis for nonverbal people.

Some nonverbal signs of schizophrenia overlap with Autistic Disorder and other Pervasive Developmental Disorders. Social withdrawal, odd behaviors, and stereotypies are common in both disorders (Fletcher et al., 2007 a, b).

Attention-Deficit Hyperactivity Disorder (ADHD)

ADHD is a common disorder indicated by inattention, distractibility, impulsiveness, overactivity, and restlessness. Diagnosis requires an onset before the age of 6, and the persistence of symptoms over time and across multiple environments. The three subtypes are: *predominantly inattentive type, predominantly hyperactive/impulsive type*, and *hyperactive/impulsive subtype*.

AHDH has been reported for children with ID (Huang & Ruedrich, 2007). Treatment is similar to that used for the general population, especially regarding the use of stimulant medications (Huang & Ruedrich, 2007).

Reiss (2008) has suggested the importance of distinguishing between ADHD, which is a mental health disorder, and normal incuriosity. Children who are incurious may become very bored in school or learning situations, not because of deficits in attention, but rather because they dislike thinking. These children might show significant attention to, say, sports, dance, social life, and other nonintellectual pursuits. Incurious children can be sloppy, late, and disorganized, not because they have abnormal hyperactivity, but rather because they value spontaneous experiences (which falls under a weak need for order). Reiss (2008) suggests that diagnosticians distinguish normal incuriosity and sloppiness from abnormal ADHD.

Conclusion

The dual diagnosis movement has broadened clinical interests in the ID field from challenging behavior to the full range of mental illnesses including anxiety disorders, affective disorders, schizophrenia, and ADHD.

Some evidence suggests that anxiety, but perhaps not anxiety disorder, is more common in the ID population. Phobias occur but rarely are treated. Researchers have not yet determined the relationship between stereotyped behavior and obsessive-compulsive disorder. Posttraumatic Stress Disorder has become a much more frequent diagnosis in both ID and non-ID populations because of the expanding definition of trauma.

Major depression in consumers usually can be diagnosed with confidence. Depressed mood tends to last a long period of time in this population and is associated with poor social skills, low levels of social support, and loneliness. Some instances of anger, irritability, and aggression may be motivated by depressed mood. We know very little about suicide in this population other than that it occurs.

Psychiatrists generally agree that schizophrenia can be diagnosed in people with mild ID who can self-report hallucination and delusions. However, most think that schizophrenia cannot be diagnosed for nonverbal individuals who have IQs under 50. ADHD has been reported for children with ID, but psychiatrists may sometimes confuse normal incuriosity for ADHD, resulting in the overdiagnosis of this disorder.

Chapter 7

Assessing Dual Diagnosis

Historically, experts distinguished between primary and secondary handicaps (Cutts, 1957; Russell & Tanguay, 1981). Is the individual primarily ID, or is the individual primarily mentally ill? Did the individual's mental illness cause ID, or did his/her ID cause the co-occurring mental illness?

The determination of a primary diagnosis had major implications for service eligibility. People diagnosed as primarily ID were served by developmental centers, whereas those diagnosed as primarily mentally ill were served by psychiatric hospitals.

In the 1970s Frank Menolascino introduced the construct of "dual diagnosis" as an alternative to the distinction between primary and secondary diagnoses. Menolascino diagnosed both disabilities and identified all important service needs. This innovation changed the aim of assessment from primary versus secondary handicaps to identifying specific psychiatric disorders. In this chapter we will consider issues relevant to such assessments.

Challenges of Psychiatric Diagnosis

Generally, the presence of ID increases the difficulty of establishing a psychiatric diagnosis. Experts have discussed the following challenges of psychiatric diagnosis in people with ID.

Limited Verbal Capacity. The presence of such psychiatric symptoms as hallucinations, delusions, and obsessional thought are most often identified from consumer self-reports. Many people with ID, however, have difficulty self-reporting their emotions, experiences, thoughts, and social relationships (Charlot, Deutsch, Hunt, Fletcher, & McIlvane, 2007; Sovner, 1986). People with IQs less than 50 have the added problem of significant language impairment and may be nonverbal.

Faked Understanding. Many people with ID try to hide their misunderstanding of questions because they do not wish to be viewed as lacking intelligence. They may agree to everything suggested by an interviewer. Diagnosticians should not be satisfied with "yes/no" responses but need to probe deeper for convincing details.

Limited Life Experience. Some behaviors that mimic psychiatric symptoms are really normal reactions to the person's life experiences. Diagnosticians need to be careful not to confuse such normal behavior for a psychiatric symptom. Szymanski (1980), for example, reported the following case vignette:

> A mildly-retarded 14 year-old boy talked during psychological testing about a girl in his head who "controlled" him. He was diagnosed as psychotic, but in psychiatric interviews no evidence of though disorder was found. The boy told, with a smile, how the girl in his head was, of course, not real but he had to invent her since, not having any friends, he needed someone to talk to (pp. 77-78).

Relevance of Psychiatric Diagnoses. Bouras, Brooks, and Dummond (1993) evaluated the extent to which conventional diagnostic criteria can be applied to people with ID. These investigators examined 356 referrals to a community psychiatric service in England. The participants were composed of 57.6 percent with mild ID, 27.4 percent with moderate ID, and 15 percent with severe ID. The psychiatrists were able to make DSM-III-R diagnoses for only 42.8 percent of the people they evaluated. In the remaining cases, though behavioral problems were evident, it was not possible to determine a specific psychiatric diagnosis.

The NADD (formerly National Association on Dual Diagnosis) convened a large group of dual diagnosis experts to suggest ways of adapting psychiatric diagnostic criteria for use with people with ID. This effort resulted in the publication of two related books (Fletcher et al., 2007a, b), which I will call the "NADD Manual." Since the manual has not yet been evaluated scientifically, we do not know the reliability of its modified diagnostic criteria.

Diagnostic Data

Psychiatric diagnoses are more reliable when they are based on multiple sources of data rather than a single source. The following data sources are often available for people with a dual diagnosis.

Case Records. Diagnosticians should read carefully the consumer's case files. These may contain previous professional reports, behavior observations, and behavior incidents. These data may provide the history of any problem behaviors.

Observations. Diagnosticians should visit the consumer's everyday environments, including classrooms and residence. Whenever practical, caregivers should observe and note the frequency, intensity, antecedents, and consequents of maladaptive behavior.

Client Interviews. Diagnosticians should spend some time interacting with the consumer. Depending on the individual's developmental level, this may include a formal interview or a play session. The diagnostician should use simple vocabulary, speak in short sentences, ask one question at a time, wait for an answer before proceeding, and check back with the individual for confirmation that he or she has correctly understood the question (Fletcher et al., 2007a, b). Szymanski (1980) has suggested the need to avoid the perception that the interview is a test.

Staff/Family Interviews. Under a promise of confidentiality, diagnosticians should interview staff and family persons individually.

Diagnostic Guidelines

Despite the limitations of psychiatric diagnosis with this population, sometimes we can make confident diagnoses by applying the following three guidelines.

1. *Diagnose patterns of behavior, not isolated symptoms.* Diagnosticians need to observe a cluster/ group of symptoms described in *DSM* [the official nomenclature of the American Psychiatric Association] or the NADD Manual.

2. *Diagnose deteriorations in functioning.* The phenomenon of *regression* can be helpful in the diagnosis of mental disorders. Suppose we need to decide if a man's unkempt appearance is a possible expression of schizophrenia or some other mental disorder. If the man's current behavior represents deterioration in behavior from prior habits, the behavior may be symptomatic of a mental disorder. If the man's current behavior does not represent deterioration from prior functioning, the behavior is not a sign of regression and schizophrenia or some other mental disorder is not suggested.

Mental illness can be diagnosed with some confidence if an entire recognizable pattern of symptoms occur in the context of deterioration from prior functioning. Diagnosticians should compare the individual's current maladaptive behaviors to the individual's past behaviors. When the death of a loved one, for example, is followed by *changes* in activity levels, *changes* in eating habits, and *changes* in sleeping habits, we have a solid basis for diagnosing affective disorder.

3. *Do not overdiagnose psychiatric disorders.* We should readily admit the limitations of current knowledge. When it is unclear whether or not a psychiatric diagnosis can be established, it is best to list maladaptive behaviors without suggesting a specific diagnosis.

Reiss Screen for Maladaptive Behavior (RSMB)

Many diagnosticians use psychiatric symptom rating scales to provide an objective source of information about consumers suspected of dual diagnosis. The first standardized instrument, still widely used, was the Reiss Screen for Maladaptive Behavior (Reiss Screen, 2009, 1988) introduced at the 1987 UIC-NIMH International Research Conference on the Mental Health Aspects of Mental Retardation held in Evanston, Illinois. This 38-item rating tool provides an objective method for asking caregivers, teachers, parents, or supervisors who should be referred for further evaluation for a possible mental health problem. The RSMB is used with people 12-years or older with severe, moderate, or mild ID. (As discussed later, a children's version is now available.)

On the Reiss Screen questionnaire, caregivers and teachers rate each of 36 maladaptive behaviors on a 3-point scale of "no problem," "problem," or "major problem." The ratings are scored into eight psychiatric scales, six maladaptive behaviors, and a 26-item total score. The eight psychiatric scales are as follows:

> Aggressive Behavior
> Autism
> Psychosis
> Paranoia
> Depression (behavioral signs)
> Depression (physical signs)
> Dependent Personality Disorder
> Avoidant Disorder

The six maladaptive behaviors, each representing a serious mental health problem, are scored separately.

> Drug/Alcohol Abuse
> Overactive
> Self-Injury
> Sexual Problem
> Stealing
> Suicidal Tendencies

The 26-item total score is a measure of severity of dual diagnosis.

Demographic Results. The Reiss Screen test manual summarizes research data on 1,456 persons collected from five national, state, and metropolitan samples (Reiss, 2009, 1988). There were few differences in maladaptive behavior between the females and males. Women had higher scores than men on the Depression (B) Scale, $F(1, 408) = 3.94$, $p < .05$. Women also scored higher than the men on the Depression (P) Scale, but the difference was not statistically significant. These findings are consistent with previous reports that depression is diagnosed more commonly among women than men (Reiss & Trenn, 1984). For all other scales, differences in average score as a function of gender were small and statistically insignificant.

People with ID scored differently across mild, moderate, and severe/ profound categories, but the differences were small. On the Aggressive Behavior Scale, people with mild and moderate ID scored minimally higher than people with severe/profound ID. The reverse was true for the Paranoia Scale, with people with mild ID scoring slightly lower than people with severe/profound ID. On the Depression (B) Scale, there was a tendency for people with severe/ profound ID to score a little bit higher than people with mild ID. On the Depression (B), Depression (P), and Dependent Personality Disorder Scales, African-Americans with ID obtained lower ratings than whites with ID.

Reliability of Scores. Various investigators calculated Cronbach's alpha coefficient of internal reliability for the 26-item total score. The results were .81 (Sturmey & Bertman, 1994), .84 (Reiss, 2009), .90 for a Dutch language version (Van Minnen et al., 1995), .90 for a Swedish language version (Gustafsson & Sonnander, 2002), and .91 for a Norwegian language version (Myrbakk & Tetzchner, 2008). With only a few exceptions, the internal reliability coefficients for the eight psychiatric scales were estimated to be above .70.

Factor Validity. The Reiss Screen is essentially a structured method of asking raters to identify those people who might need further evaluation for mental health services. Since the raters do not know the symptoms of mental disorders, the Reiss Screen provides them with a comprehensive list of symptoms that are defined in non-technical language. The symptoms are presented alphabetically with no suggestion as to how they might cluster into disorders.

The factor validity of the Reiss Screen is the degree to which nonprofessional raters correctly identify the symptoms that go with one another. People with psychoses, for example, tend to experience both hallucinations and delusions. Yet many teachers, caretakers, and work supervisors do not know this. The only way they could consistently tell us which psychiatric symptoms go together is by validly observing people who have psychiatric conditions and reporting correctly the symptoms that are present.

The first version of the Reiss Screen consisted of a 40-item scale that was administered to 511 people with all levels of ID and varying in age from 12 to 70. These data were submitted to a principal component analysis that was interpreted into seven clinically meaningful scales. The five items with the highest loading on each factor were selected to form the scales for the Reiss Screen. Subsequently, an Autism scale and two experimental items were added.

Havercamp and Reiss (1997) executed a confirmatory factor study with 448 research participants with mild, moderate, and severe/profound ID located throughout the United States and Canada. Based on RMSEA, ECVI, NNFI, and NFI statistics, the results demonstrated a "reasonable fit" of the 8-factor Reiss Screen model. The 1996 confirmatory factor analysis showed that the eight-factor solution, developed in exploratory factor studies executed in 1987, still provided a reasonable fit to 1996 data. The factorial stability was obtained despite the large number of factors in the solution and the presence of overlapping factors. These results provided evidence for the factorial validity of the Reiss Screen.

Face Validity. Each item on the Reiss Screen measures an important mental health problem for which services should be provided; no test item refers to a relatively ordinary or minor psychological problem. Consider, for example, the ratings of "major problem" for aggression or sadness. When people are rated as having a "major problem" with aggressive behavior, it means that they are aggressive to the point that they lose jobs, require increased supervision, or are placed in restrictive environments or special school programs. When people are rated as having a "major problem" with sadness, it means that their unhappiness is so severe they have difficulty executing the chores of everyday life including work, school, or ordinary interpersonal relationships.

Concurrent Validity. The Reiss Screen 26-item total score is highly correlated with the total scores on other dual diagnosis measures, regardless of whether those other measures were intended for use with people with mild ID versus severe ID. As a result, it is not necessary to have separate scales for the various ID severity levels. Regarding people with mild ID, Davidson (1988) obtained a .83 correlation between the total score on the Reiss Screen and the "ratings-by-others" version of the Psychopathology Inventory of Mentally Retarded Adults (PIMRA; Matson, Kazdin, & Senatore, 1984). Monroe (1987) obtained a correlation of .78 between the total score on the Reiss Screen with the total score on the Adaptive Behavior Scales Part II (ABS-II; ABC Part II; Nihira, Leland, & Lambert, 1993). Walsh and Shenouda (1999) administered the Reiss Screen, AAMR Adaptive Behavior Scales Part II, and the Aberrant Behavior Checklist (ABC; Aman, Singh, Stewart, & Field, 1985) to 284 dual diagnosis clinic clients living in community residences. The Reiss Screen total score correlated .65 with ABS Part II Disturbing Interpersonal Behavior.

Regarding people with severe ID, Sturmey and Bertman (1993) found a .54 correlation between the total score on the Reiss Screen and the total score on the ABC (ABC; Aman, Singh, Stewart, & Field, 1985). Walsh and Shenouda (1999) found that the Reiss Screen total score correlated .67 with ABC irritability and .45 with ABC lethargy.

Criterion Validity of Total Score. On average the Reiss Screen 26-item total score is a full standard deviation higher for people with a dual diagnosis versus those with ID but no mental illness. Reiss (1988) reported that 167 participants with no psychiatric diagnoses in their case file had a mean total score of 9.9, whereas 139 participants with a psychiatric diagnosis in their case file had a mean total score of 14.9, $F (1, 305) = 32.94$, $p < .001$. For a sample diagnosed by clinical psychologists unaware of Reiss Screen scores, the mean Reiss Screen total score was 10.9 for 38 participants judged to have a dual diagnosis versus 4.4 for 21 participants judged to be mentally healthy, $F (1,58) = 18.19$, $p < .001$. On the Dutch version of the Reiss Screen, Van Minnen and Hoogduin (1995) found that consumers with psychopathology (dual diagnosis) scored more than a full standard deviation higher on the total score than did those with no mental health disorder. These findings provide evidence for the criterion validity of the total score as an indicator of the likelihood that a person has a dual diagnosis.

Criterion Validity of Eight Psychiatric Scales. Myrbakk and Tetzchner (2008, p. 54) found that the Reiss Screen's eight psychiatric scales are valid indicators of dual diagnosis generally but not of specific psychiatric disorders. These investigators, however, did not study a sample large enough to support such a broad conclusion. In order to determine the concordance between the Reiss Screen depression scales and psychiatric diagnoses of depression, for example, the sample must include a sufficient number of individuals who were diagnosed as depressed. Myrbakk and Tetzchner (2008) did not report the numbers of persons in their study with each psychiatric diagnosis; it is possible that the RSMB depression scale did not indicate psychiatric diagnosis of depression because the sample had few depressed patients.

The original scale development studies reported in the Reiss Screen test manual (Reiss, 1988, 2009) showed substantial concordance rates between the eight psychiatric scales and psychiatric diagnoses. In studies with a total N of 564, the RSMB psychiatric scales were significantly correlated with psychiatric diagnoses in the following three ways.

> *Mentally Healthy vs. Mentally Ill*: People with a dual diagnosis scored higher on all eight Reiss Screen psychiatric scales than did people with ID but no psychiatric disorder.

Between Diagnostic Groups: The highest average scores on each psychiatric scale were obtained by groups diagnosed with a disorder relevant to that scale. People who had a psychotic disorder, for example, scored higher on the RSMB psychosis scales than did people with dual diagnoses other than psychosis.

Within Diagnostic Groups: Individuals had higher RSMB scores on scales relevant to their diagnoses versus scales not relevant to their diagnoses. People with psychotic disorders, for example, scored higher on the psychosis scale than they did on the other RSMB psychiatric disorders.

Validity of Cutoff Scores. The Reiss Screen recommends referral for further mental health evaluations based on a system of 14 cutoff scores, including seven cutoff scores for the psychiatric scales (all except Autism), six cutoff scores for the special maladaptive behavior items, and one cutoff score for the 26-item total score. A positive test result means that the person is likely to need a mental health service. A negative test result means that the person is likely to be mentally healthy. The results of one study suggested that 86.7% of the "positives" had mental health problems and that 58.6% of the negatives had no mental health problems, chi-square = 12.93, df = 1, p < .005. A second study suggested that the validity of the cutoff scores was 81.1 percent of cases.

For a sample of 21 randomly selected individuals, Gustafsson and Sonnander (2003) found that 80% of persons diagnosed by psychiatrists tested positive for dual diagnosis on the Reiss Screen, and that 83% of persons evaluated by psychiatrists to be mentally healthy tested negative on the Reiss Screen. The study showed only one false positive and three false negatives out of 21 cases.

Because negative test results are not always valid, the Reiss Screen should not be used as a basis for ignoring non-test evidence of mental health problems. When there is other evidence of possible mental health problems, the person should be referred for professional evaluation regardless of the results on the Reiss Screen.

Cross-Cultural Validity. The Reiss Screen has been administered successfully in a variety of languages and cultures, including French-speaking Canada (Lecavalier & Tasse, 2001), India (Kishore, Nizamie, & Nizamie, 2005; Kishore, Nizamie, Nizamie, & Jahan, 2004), Netherlands (Van Minnen, Savelsberg, & Hoogduin, 1995), Norway (Myrbakk & Tetzchner, 2008), Spain (Sacristan, 1987), and Sweden (e.g., Gustafsson et al., 2002).

Sacristan (1987) translated the Reiss Screen into Spanish and assessed 434 people with ID from institutions and clinics located in Spain.

He submitted these data to an exploratory factor analysis and reproduced the eight scales, providing evidence for the cross-cultural relevance of the Reiss Screen.

Myrbakk and Tetzchner (2008) reported substantial validity for the cutoff scores in a Norwegian translated version of Reiss Screen. These studies support the cross-cultural relevance of the RSMB.

Gustafsson and Sonnander (2002) submitted data from 200 randomly selected people with and without mental health problems to a principal component analysis. The analysis yielded seven interpretable components with eigenvalues > 1 that explained 67% of the variance. The seven scales could be interpreted in terms of the same clinical categories Reiss (1988) reported.

Reiss Scales for Children's Dual Diagnosis (RSDD)

This instrument is a children's version of the Reiss Screen. Caregivers, teachers, or parents rate the degree to which each of 60 symptoms is currently no problem, a problem, or a major problem. The instrument is scored into 10 psychiatric scales, 10 maladaptive behaviors, and a total score. The 10 psychometric scales are:

> Anger/Self-Control
> Anxiety Disorder
> Attention Deficit
> Autism/Pervasive Development Disorder
> Conduct Disorder
> Depression
> Poor Self-Esteem
> Psychosis
> Somatoform Behavior
> Withdrawn/Isolated

The 10 maladaptive behaviors are:

> Crying Spells
> Enuresis/Encopresis
> Hallucinations
> Involuntary Motor Movements
> Lies
> Obese
> Pica
> Sets Fires
> Sexual Problem
> Verbally Abusive

As with the Reiss Screen, the RSDD should be completed by two or more raters for each individual. The purpose of obtaining two ratings rather than one is to increase the reliability of the results. All rating scales are more reliable when they are based on average scores from multiple raters as compared to when they reflect the opinions of only one person. The raters complete the RSDD on their own and without consulting with others. Much of the advantage of using average scores from two raters is lost when the raters talk with one another about their ratings. The raters should be told that their ratings are confidential.

The RSDD test manual summarizes data for 583 children and adolescents (Reiss & Valenti-Hein, 1990). Cronbach's alpha coefficients were estimated at .91 for the total score and between .63 and .86 for the ten psychometric scales. These findings provided an adequate to high degree of internal reliability.

Children with a dual diagnosis scored more than a full standard deviation higher on the RSDD total score than did children with ID but no mental health disorder (Reiss & Valenti-Hein, 1990). The overall accuracy of the system of cutoff scores was estimated at 74.7 percent (Reiss & Valenti-Hein, 1990). These findings provided evidence for the criterion validity of the RSDD.

Diagnostic Instruments

A number of scales were constructed to assess specific mental health disorders in persons with ID. These measures are potentially suitable for research purposes, or to help confirm a specific diagnosis. Generally, though, the measures are in need of additional research regarding reliability, validity, and applicability to the ID population.

Anxiety and Mood Disorders. King, Ollendick, Gullone, Cummins, and Josephs (1990) discussed the assessment of fears in people with ID. They suggested focusing on the individual's actual behavior while being alert for acquiescence responses. They suggested that clinicians use the Revised Fear Survey Schedule for Children (FSSC-R; Ollendick, 1988) and the Louisville Fear Survey for Children (Miller, Barrett, Hampe, & Noble, 1971).

Lindsay and Michie (1988) adapted the Zung Self-Rating Anxiety Scale (Zung, 1971) for use with people with ID. The research participants were 29 adults with mild to moderate ID. Various response formats were evaluated, but internal reliabilities were low. A marginal split-half reliability of .69 was found for a no/yes response format.

Meins (1993) administered a German-translated, modified version of the Child's Depression Inventory (CDI) to 798 consumers aged 20 or older. Approximately 56.9 percent of the sample lived in community-based residences. The alpha coefficient for the 26-item instrument was estimated at .86. Follow-up psychiatric evaluations indicated that high scores were associated with a diagnosis of mood disorders including major depression, dysthymia, and adjustment disorder.

Meins's modification of the CDI was designed primarily for adults with mild ID. The instrument appears less applicable for people with more severe ID. Some items (e.g., "pessimism," "belief that one is ugly") may not be applicable to people who are nonverbal.

Reynolds and Baker (1988) developed a 32-item instrument, called the Self-Report Depression Questionnaire (SRDQ), for measuring depression in persons with mild ID. The item content relates to the physical, cognitive, and behavioral symptoms of depression. The items are read to the person in an interview format, and the individual responds by indicating on a three-point, anchored scale how frequently he/she experiences each symptom.

Reynolds and Baker's (1988) initial research sample consisted of 103 persons with mild ID between the ages of 21 and 72 years. Approximately 14 percent of the sample was unable to pass a pretest that evaluated whether or not they could comprehend the items. For the remaining individuals, a coefficient alpha of .90 was found, suggesting a high degree of internal reliability. Test-retest reliability over an 11-week period was .63. The SRDQ correlated significantly with the Hamilton Depression Rating Scale.

The SRDQ is a promising, carefully constructed measure from an author who is recognized for assessment work with adolescent school populations. The instrument, however, has not attracted a following, perhaps because of an absence of follow-up research.

Esbensen, Rojahn, Aman, and Ruedrich (2003) constructed the 55-item "Anxiety, Depression, and Mood Scale" (ADAMS) to assess mood disorders. They reported data from three samples with a total N = 662. They confirmed a 5-factor model with scales for "Manic/Hyperactive Behavior," "Depressed Mood," "Social Avoidance," "General Anxiety," and "Compulsive Behavior." The alpha coefficients of internal reliability ranged from .75 to .83, and interrater reliability from .37 to .62. They reported evidence of discriminate validity, which was limited by overlapping symptoms.

Charlot at al. (2007) constructed the Mood and Anxiety Semi-Structured (MASS) interview for people with a dual diagnosis. The structured interview format represents a different method of assessing the mood of persons with ID versus the previous method of rating scales. The results were validated against psychiatric diagnoses and widely used rating scales.

Miller, Fee, and Netterville (2004) compared the psychometric properties of six ADHD scales. Although the study was well executed and addressed an important issue, the sample was too small (n =49) to support even preliminary conclusions. Generally, an absolute minimum of 100 participants is necessary for a psychometric study to have statistical significance.

Conclusion

Psychiatrists have two primary strategies for diagnosing mental health disorders in people with ID. One, they can diagnose based on evidence of abnormal psychological development. Here the psychiatrist compares the individual's behavior to norms or with theories of normal development. Two, they can diagnose based on evidence of significant deterioration in functioning, called regression. Here the psychiatrist compares the individual's current behavior to the individual's premorbid behavior. When behavior is diagnosed based on evidence of regression, it may not be essential to know what normal development is, only that the individual is now functioning at significantly lower levels than before.

Psychiatric diagnosis is especially challenging for people with ID because of their limited verbal capacity, tendency to fake understanding of questions, and limited life experiences. We have some preliminary evidence of significant unreliability of psychiatric diagnosis. Recent NADD guidelines aimed at adapting diagnostic criteria for use with people with ID are based on consensus expert opinion.

Psychiatric diagnoses need to be executed carefully based on multiple sources of data including case records, behavior observations, client interviews, staff/family interviews, and the results of various tools and rating instruments. Diagnosticians should not diagnose based on a single symptom but instead should diagnose based on patterns of symptoms, especially patterns of symptoms that present as a deterioration in functioning from premorbid levels.

The construction of reliable and valid screening instruments, such as the Reiss Screen for Maladaptive Behavior, made it possible to identify service needs in a cost effective manner. The results of large population screening provided evidence of the need for services. During the 1990s hundreds of new clinics and supports were created in the United States, Canada, and United Kingdom. Today, the Reiss Screen, and its companion instrument for children, the Reiss Scales, is still widely used. These instruments screen for dual diagnosis in three ways: the 26-item total score assesses severity of maladaptive behavior; the eight psychiatric scales assess type of mental health disorder; and the six maladaptive behavior items assess rare but very serious problems.

Future researchers should construct reliable and valid tools for specific diagnostic categories. The ones that have been reported thus far are promising but generally are still in a preliminary stage of development.

Chapter 8

Abnormal Motives

E ven though researchers have extensively studied the cognitive, be-havioral, psychodynamic, and neurophysiologic aspects of mental illness, they have paid much less attention to abnormal motivation. Yet this aspect of abnormal behavior is potentially an important organizing theme of the various other aspects of abnormal behavior. In this chapter, we will discuss four abnormal motives: excessive vengeance, excessive need for attention, anxiety sensitivity, and excessive sensitivity for failure.

Excessive Vengeance

The Frustration-Aggression hypothesis has two tenets (Dollard, Doob, Miller, Mowrer, & Sears, 1939; Miller, 1941):

1. All frustration inevitably leads to some type of aggressive response.
2. All aggression occurs in reaction to some frustration.

Miller (1941) clarified this hypothesis by saying that, "Frustration produces instigations to a number of different types of responses, one of which is instigation to some form of aggression" (p. 338).

In the 1960s Bandura and his colleague showed that aggression is not always preceded by frustration (Bandura & Walters, 1963). In the Ban-dura studies, young children either did or did not view films of an aggres-sive model striking a "Bobo" doll. When the children subsequently were left alone in a room with the very same Bobo doll, the ones who viewed the aggressive model were themselves aggressive.

The Bandura studies showed that aggression could be taught to peo-ple who did not have a history of temper problems and who had not been frustrated. Bandura and Walters (1963) wrote, "One can readily produce a highly aggressive child by merely exposing him to successful aggressive models and rewarding the child intermittently for aggressive behavior, while keeping frustration at a very low level" (p. 159).

The Bandura studies encouraged a learning theory approach to aggres-sion. This approach focused on situational stimuli and paid little or no atten-tion to the role of personality variables and frustration of needs. Behavior-ists concluded that aggression is a learned behavior, not a personality trait.

As it turns out, however, aggression is both a personality trait and a learned behavior. Eron and Huesmann (1990) conducted some of the most important studies of aggression over the lifespan. In research recognized with distinguished awards from the American Psychological Association, they investigated aggression in 632 people. They first observed these individuals in third grade and then made repeated observations for 40 years. They found that aggressive children become aggressive adults, and that nonviolent children became nonviolent adults. Here is how they summarized their research findings:

> Aggression ... has the hallmarks of a deeply ingrained personality trait. It is related to genetic and physiological factors; it emerges early in life but is influenced and shaped by a child's experiences; it is consistently associated with gender and is stable or predictable over time and across situations.

The Eron and Huessman results have been replicated in longitudinal research conducted in various countries (Eron & Huesmann, 1990). These studies followed research participants for 24, 11, and 18 years, respectively, in Britain, Finland, and Sweden. The results of these studies proved the stability of aggressive behavior over the lifespan. If we look at the amount of aggression Sam Smith, a typical person, shows from age 6 to age 60, it rises until ages 20-30, and then declines. If we look at how aggressive Sam Smith is compared with same-aged peers, Sam's aggressiveness changes very little as the years pass.

The stability of aggressive behavior over time is evident in people with a dual diagnosis. I consulted, for example, on the case of a man with ID who was on death row for murder and whose case file was remarkable for its consistency. When this person was in elementary school, he was repeatedly expelled for fighting. He was arrested a number of times as a teenager for assault. When he was 15, his school psychologist predicted he would someday commit a murder. At age 16 a psychiatrist was so afraid of him he refused to conduct an interview. The murder for which the man was convicted occurred when he was 18.

Many observers have noticed that frustration /irritability increases challenging behavior in people predisposed to such behavior. The Eron findings that aggression is stable over the lifespan, and the Dollard et al. findings that frustration often leads to aggression, suggest that minimizing frustration might minimize episodes of challenging behavior in highly aggressive people. The Bandura findings suggest that minimizing observations of aggressive models also may minimize episodes of challenging behavior.

Anger and Mental Illness. High need for vengeance is sometimes associated with anger, resentment, or even hatred. These emotions play prominent roles in certain types of mental illnesses, especially paranoia, schizophrenia, depression, and personality disorder.

People with paranoia, for example, think that others are out to get them. They may feel they need to keep up their guard lest others take advantage or exploit them. They tend to become angry over minor injustices and may feel that life has been unfair to them. They are sometimes quick to take offense at the slightest provocation, making mountains out of molehills. They may misinterpret, for example, a minor disagreement of opinion as a sign of disloyalty or as a personal threat. Uncompromising and unforgiving, they are driven by a desire to get even with their real or imagined enemies.

Inhibitors of Aggression. Evolutionary biologist de Waal (1989) has recognized both primal instigators (e.g., having something taken away, loss/threat to status) and primal inhibitors (e.g., apologizing) of aggressive behavior. He believes that aggression, which is shown by all primates, is deeply rooted in human nature. Primates are aggressive only to a certain extent, however, and they also exhibit forgiveness and peacekeeping behavior (Aureli & de Waal, 2000). De Waal has encouraged efforts to use peacekeeping behavior more effectively to manage people's aggressive tendencies.

Reiss's (2008) model of human needs recognizes both instigators and inhibitors of aggressive behavior. High valuation of vengeance, which is motivation to confront others, instigates aggression, while high valuations of helps others and tranquility inhibit aggression. Helps others may inhibit aggression by inducing guilt, whereas tranquility may inhibit aggression by inducing fears of being hurt in a fight.

Reiss's model predicts aggressive behavior based on the individual's combination of needs regarding vengeance, helps others, and tranquility. A person with high needs for both vengeance and tranquility, for example, may attack weak targets who pose little threat of striking back successfully. In this way the individual gratifies his/her need for confrontation yet still satisfies the need for safety. For a person with high valuation for both vengeance and helps others, the individual's compassion (which falls under the need to help others) may inhibit the person's aggressive tendencies.

Need for Excessive Attention

When I was a clinical intern at the Harvard University's Department of Child Psychiatry, I treated Annette, who was a child with autism and challenging behavior. I will review her case history, focusing on her seemingly insatiable needs for attention and order.

Annette was admitted to a large residential program when she was six years old. During her first two years living at the developmental center, she was happy and cooperative. At about that time a member of the institution's professional staff developed an interest in her and regularly took Annette to visit parks, movies, and restaurants. Annette looked forward to these visits and developed a close emotional bond with the staff member. Unfortunately, the visits ended abruptly when the professional staff person took a job in another city. Following that loss, Annette started to scream and have frequent tantrums.

Annette's screaming was accompanied by self-injury. She scratched her neck and rubbed her underarms over her knees, causing abrasions in the skin. The wounds were so deep that her physician was concerned about possible infection.

Annette's tantrums were functionally related to attention, and her need for attention seemed insatiable. She only screamed when adults were nearby and could see her. If a caregiver walked away from her while she was screaming, she followed still screaming.

Annette demanded a high degree of order in her environment. She had tantrums, for example, when her daily schedule was not followed or her routines were interrupted. When having a tantrum, moreover, she would raise her hands to cover her ears, look around, and engage in non-stop screaming.

Using applied behavior analysis (ABA), I was able to produce dramatic, temporary improvements in Annette's behavior. My ABA program required caregivers to ignore Annette as soon as she started to scream, but praise her when she was calm. Within a few weeks of this treatment, Annette, who previously had not spoken in years, declared one day, "I do not want to scream." The screaming episodes became infrequent, and Annette's wounds healed. The child began to use simple language to communicate her needs.

Unfortunately, the dramatic improvements seen with the ABA treatment did not last. Shortly after the treatment was terminated, Annette again started to scream and abuse herself. The enduring problem was that Annette wanted much more attention than most children do. Although she received attention for appropriate behavior, the *amount* of attention she received did not satisfy her. She resorted to challenging behavior because those behaviors produced a much greater amount of attention than did appropriate behaviors.

In order to understand how need for a high amount of attention might lead to inappropriate behavior, consider the hypothetical example of two boys, Sam and Joe, both of whom are students in Miss Smith's fourth grade class. Let's assume that Sam needs only an average amount of attention but that Joe needs a great deal of attention.

When Sam and Joe behave themselves in the classroom, Miss Smith occasionally praises them for their good behavior. Since Sam has only a modest need for attention, he is satisfied by how much attention he receives from Miss Smith when he behaves himself. Consequently, he continues to behave appropriately. Joe, however, is not satisfied by the amount of attention he receives from Miss Smith when he is "good." He requires much more attention to satiate his need. He misbehaves, perhaps outrageously, as a means of getting a great deal of attention from Miss Smith.

In a sense, Joe is "addicted" to attention. He craves it, not just every once in a while, but seemingly every day. He cannot be talked out of this "addiction" because there is little he wants more than a great deal of attention. Even if Miss Smith or his parents punish him for inappropriate behavior, Joe would rather accept the punishment – itself a form of attention -- and continue to seek a great of attention than to settle for moderate amounts of attention. Effective treatment of Joe requires reducing the intensity of his craving of attention.

Communication theory. The construct of "addiction to attention" provides a basis for reinterpreting some of the results explained by Carr and Durand's (1985a, 1985b) communication theory. This theory holds that some nonverbal consumers resort to challenging behavior as a means of communicating their needs, especially their need for attention. In contrast, the construct "addiction to attention" implies that challenging behavior is motivated by an excessive need for attention.

Carr and Durand taught children with challenging behavior to communicate their need for attention by asking, "Am I doing a good job?" Although this reduced the frequency of the children's challenging behavior, it led to excessive prompting for teaching attention. Carr and Durand replaced one inappropriate behavior (tantrums) with another (excessive prompting). Successful treatment of the children's tantrums may have required reductions in their need for excessive attention, as opposed to changes in what was functionally related to attention seeking.

Anxiety Sensitivity (Excessive Need for Tranquility)

Imagine: The Chicago Cubs are playing the California Angels for their first ever World Series championship. Each team has won three games, and the series now hangs on who wins the seventh and final game. The Cubs are on the field with the score tied 3-3 with two outs and bases loaded in the bottom of the ninth. The count to the batter is 3 balls and 2 strikes. If the next pitch is a ball, the Cubs will lose the game and the World Series;

if it is a strike, they will get to play an extra inning. The manager signals to the bullpen to send in a relief pitcher to the throw what he hopes will be the final pitch of the inning. Millions of Chicagoans anxiously await the relief pitcher's arrival at the pitching mound. The tension is felt by nearly all participants and observers.

Since stress is unpleasant, why does the relief pitcher walk to the mound to throw the last pitch? Why not run away to reduce the stress? Bandura (1977) explained that the pitcher has confidence that he will strike out the batter. The pitcher, because he believes in his own mastery of the necessary skills, is imagining the glory of success, which greatly reduces the stress and worry from the possibility of failure. According to Bandura, self-efficacy explains why people walk into stressful situations rather than run away.

Although mastery/self-efficacy can help people overcome their fears, it is hard to believe that professional ball players do not understand the possibility of failure. Even self-confident pitchers must realize there is a very real chance they will throw a bad pitch and have to live with scorn and shame the rest of their lives. Self-efficacy may help self-confident people manage stress, but self-efficacy alone does not explain why people walk into stressful situations on an everyday basis.

In 1985 Richard McNally and I proposed the idea of anxiety sensitivity to explain why people often approach stressful situations rather than avoid them (Reiss & McNally, 1985). Anxiety sensitivity implies that relief pitchers walk into stressful situations, not only because they have self-confidence, but also because they know that stress is a temporary and usually harmless experience.

A small minority of people are highly sensitive to anxiety, meaning they think stress is harmful to their health or well being (McNally, 2002). These people interpret the body signs of stress -- stomach butterflies, shaking, sweating, pounding heart, dry mouth -- as signs of an impending heart attack or mental illness. If a relief pitcher were to have high anxiety sensitivity, for example, he might faint when the manager called him into the game or "choke" (let stress throw him off his game) when pitching under pressure. The reason you do not see this happen very often is because many people with high anxiety sensitivity avoid competitive sports.

Anxiety sensitivity is assessed in adults and in children by simple questionnaires called, the *Anxiety Sensitivity Index* (ASI) and the *Child Anxiety Sensitivity Index* (CASI). I wrote the original ASI in 1983 in order to test my expectancy model of fear (Reiss, 1980, 1991; Reiss & McNally, 1985). Wendy Silverman, Rolf Peterson, and others developed the Child-hood Anxiety Sensitivity Index (CASI; Silverman, Flesig, Rabian, & Peterson, 1991). The main difference between the ASI and CASI is in the simplicity of the items and ratings. Professors Wendy Silverman and Carl Weems conducted influential validity studies on the CASI.

Thus far more than 1,200 studies on anxiety sensitivity have been published and the construct has been translated into many languages. The ASI/CASI are used worldwide to help diagnose panic disorder, posttraumatic stress disorder, chronic pain, substance abuse, and childhood anxiety disorders. Further, these instruments are used in studies on anxiety disorders and to evaluate treatment progress and outcomes with anxiety patients.

ASI scores are strongly associated with the occurrence, frequency, and intensity of panic attacks. The highest ASI scores are shown by people with panic disorder, followed by people with frequent panic attacks, followed by people with infrequent panic attacks, followed by those with no panic experiences (Reiss et al., 2008).

Military psychologists have shown interest in the role of anxiety sensitivity in maladjustment and in posttraumatic stress disorder. Since soldiers need to cope with the intense stress of combat, basic training at the U. S. Air Force Academy is designed to be highly stressful. The cadets are not allowed to call home during training, they are awakened in the middle of the night and made to go on marches, and they are driven almost to the point of breaking. Although the vast majority of the cadets make it through basic training without psychological difficulty, a few have problems. If we can understand why some cadets do not cope well with basic training, we might gain insights into how stress affects our behavior.

Schmidt, Lerew, and Jackson (1997) conducted two studies of anxiety sensitivity and panic during military basic training. In the first study, 1,401 young adults were prospectively followed over a 5-week period at the U.S. Air Force Academy. The results revealed that a recruit's ASI score predicted spontaneous panic attacks during basic training. Approximately 20% of those scoring in the upper deciles on the ASI experienced a panic attack during the 5-week follow-up period compared with only 6% for the remainder of the sample. The ASI also predicted anxiety symptoms and anxiety functional impairment.

Schmidt, Lerew, and Jackson (1999) replicated the main findings of their previous study with a new group of 1,296 military recruits at the U.S. Air Force Academy. Consistent with the initial study, ASI scores predicted spontaneous panic attacks after controlling for a history of panic attacks and trait anxiety. They concluded that it was the cadet's sensitivity to anxiety, not just the amount of anxiety the cadet experienced, that best predicted psychological maladjustment. *If you want to know who will have trouble coping with stress, it is more important to know what the person thinks will happen to him or her as a consequence of experiencing stress, than to know how much stress the person experiences.*

Pain Intolerance. Anxiety sensitivity is associated with pain intolerance (Plehn, Peterson and Williams, 1998). Asmundson (1999) studied chronic pain patients and found that high ASI scores were correlated with high subjective distress and poor self-control. Asmundson and Taylor (1996) found that both subjective pain severity and anxiety sensitivity may be related to the fear of pain.

Schmidt and Cook (1999) examined the role of anxiety sensitivity in pain during a cold presser challenge task in a study with 22 panic disorder patients and 22 nonclinical matched controls. They found that ASI scores predicted both pain and anxiety responses to the cold presser task.

Alcohol Consumption Problems. Because people with high anxiety sensitivity cannot stand the bodily sensations of stress, they may turn to drinking as a means of blunting the intensity of bodily sensations (Reiss et al., 2008). Drinking problems develop because alcohol is being used as a tranquilizer.

Genetics. Anxiety sensitivity has a complex etiology that is poorly understood. Twin researchers have found that anxiety sensitivity is related to additive genetic influences in anxiety outcomes (Stein, Jang, & Livesley, 1999). Taylor, Jang, Stewart, and Stein (2008) administered the ASI to 245 monozygotic and 193 dizygotic twin pairs, comparing 658 women and 218 men. Heritability in women significantly increased with ASI scores, indicating that severe forms of anxiety sensitivity, compared to milder forms, are more strongly influenced by genetic factors.

Stein, Schork, & Gelenter (2007) reported that the serotonin transporter gene promoter polymorphism (5-HTTLPR) interacted with childhood maltreatment to predict anxiety sensitivity. S/S individuals (those with two copies of the "short" form of this gene) had higher levels of emotional abuse and were more likely to have higher levels of anxiety sensitivity.

Excessive Sensitivity to Failure

The "self-esteem" movement in education advocates protecting children from the psychologically damaging effects of failure. Some youth basketball programs, for example, do not keep score so the team that loses will not feel bad. Many schools generously award high grades and second or even third opportunities to redo tests or terms papers.

Park (1998) studied how children react to failure experiences. She examined two possible predictors of test anxiety: "failure frequency" versus "sensitivity to failure." Failure frequency is simply how often a child gets a failing grade on tests; sensitivity to failure is the pressure a child puts on himself or herself to do well. The child who gets good grades while think-ing that failure would be a social catastrophe has high failure sensitivity but low failure frequency. The child who fails tests often but does not care has low failure sensitivity but high failure frequency.

As demonstrated in an Ohio State University master's thesis, children who had failed tests frequently approached new tests with only slightly more anxiety than did the average student. In contrast, the children who put a lot of pressure on themselves to succeed -- the children with high failure sensitivity who thought that failing tests is a personal catastrophe -- approached exams with a great deal of anxiety. It was how children inter-preted failure, not how often they failed, that was highly predictive of how anxious they were when they took exams (Park, 1998).

Park's findings have important implications for education and treat-ment strategies. Protecting children from failure experiences is unlikely to lead to psychologically healthy development. Instead, children need to be taught healthy ways of interpreting the meaning of personal failure. They need to know that it is unfortunate, but not a personal catastrophe, to fail. Success is desirable but not essential for happiness.

Prevention

Based on the professional experiences of scores of executive coaches and counselors, I suspect that a person's human needs predict future be-havior in natural environments, something that is very difficult to do. The ASI, for example, is a valid predictor of future Panic Disorder even for people who have had no past panic attacks. Here are some additional im-pressions that should be evaluated in future research:

> A very strong need for Acceptance may predict psychiatric dis-orders and adjustment problems.

> A very strong need for Attention may predict future conduct problems.

> A very strong need for Tranquility may predict anxiety disor-ders, substance abuse, and certain chronic pain conditions.

> A very weak need for Helps Others, combined with a strong need for Vengeance, may predict antisocial behavior including aggression, stealing, and cheating.

By identifying abnormal motives early on, researchers have new opportunities to study the prevention of maladaptive behaviors and psychiatric disorders.

Treatment and Maintenance

Intervention methods are needed for treating abnormal needs. Here are some speculative ideas for future research.

> Cognitive-behavior therapists may attempt to change abnormal motives by altering beliefs about the consequences of those motives. In anxiety sensitivity, for example, cognitive therapists now aim to alter the client's belief that anxiety sensations are dangerous. In another example, cognitive therapists teach skills aimed at boosting a person's self-confidence, thereby lowering the individual's need for an abnormal degree of external acceptance from others. Benson's (1990) anger management program for persons with ID provides training aimed at teaching self-control of inappropriate anger responses.

> Psychotropic medications may alter some abnormal motives at least temporarily, but we need much more research before firm conclusions may be drawn. Some anti-anxiety agents, for example, may lessen anxiety sensitivity. Some anti-depressants lessen the need for Acceptance. Researchers need to evaluate drugs to study the effects of medications on abnormal motives as well as on traditional psychiatric symptoms.

> Using the principle of greater motives (Reiss, 2000), behavior therapists might increase the strength of a low-priority reinforcing stimulus by pairing it in Pavlovian trials with a high-priority reinforcing stimulus. Consider the example of a child with isolate behavior, a low need for social contact, and a high need for physical activity. Therapists might be able to increase the motivational strength of socializing by pairing social experiences with opportunities for physical activity.

Conclusion

Nearly all people with a dual diagnosis exhibit abnormal needs. Yet very little attention has been paid to such needs and how they play out in mental illnesses. This chapter provided a rare discussion of four abnormal needs: trait aggression, need for excessive attention, anxiety sensitivity, and sensitivity to failure.

Since frustration often precedes aggression, minimizing frustration is a strategy for minimizing aggression. Under Reiss's (2008) model, trait aggression is the result of two kinds of forces, called instigators and inhibitors. The primary instigator is an excessive need for vengeance, whereas the primary inhibitors are strong needs to help others and experience tranquility. In other words, revenge instigates trait aggression, but morals and timidity inhibit it. This model may predict how aggressive somebody is now or will be in the future.

A need for excessive amounts of attention may instigate or predict persistent conduct problems including challenging behavior. Although individuals with ID receive attention when they behave appropriately, they receive much more attention when they behave inappropriately. Consequently, people who need excessive attention may embrace conduct problems (tantrums, self-injury) as the only means they have for receiving the *amount* of attention they desire.

People with high anxiety sensitivity are at risk for panic disorder, post-traumatic stress disorder, alcoholism, and in certain medical conditions, chronic pain. This knowledge can be used in the early identification of high risk groups. Knowledge of anxiety sensitivity also aids in the assessment and treatment of various anxiety disorders.

Park (1998) demonstrated that it is not how often we fail, but how much pressure we put on ourselves to succeed, that matters most in terms of test anxiety

Chapter 9

Crisis Intervention

How could we use knowledge of a person's needs to minimize the individual's frustration and, thus, minimize psychiatric symptoms, especially challenging behavior? In this chapter we will discuss this issue in detail, learning numerous practical suggestions for preventing behavior outbursts called "crises."

As in Chapter 4, we will use the terminology of Green, Red, and Yellow priorities.

> *Green priority* indicates a stronger-than-average need (upper 20% when compared with the general population);

> *Red priority* indicates a weaker-than-average need (lower 20% when compared with the general population);

> *Yellow priority* indicates average need (includes 60% of the general population.).

We may ignore Yellow needs because these are usually gratified in the course of everyday life without special effort. Green and Red needs, on the other hand, must be attended to because they require special lifestyle adjustments to be gratified on a regular basis and, thus, increase the risk of frustration. We must keep in mind that Red needs, despite their being "weak," are just as important for preventing frustration as are Green needs. (The difference is often only semantic. A Red Need for Social Contact, for example, is the same as a strong need for solitude.)

Need for Acceptance

This need motivates reactions to criticism, rejection, and failure and is closely associated with self-concept issues including self esteem.

Green Acceptance. People with this need may be insecure, lack self-confidence, and/or have low self-esteem. More than their peers, people with Green Acceptance tend to have difficulty coping with being evaluated. Green Acceptance is often associated with poor self-esteem. Some (not all) may be negative thinkers who blame themselves when things go wrong. Some (not all) may have a tendency to be down in the dumps. Others may be indecisive or pessimistic.

Green Acceptance is associated with increased risk of psychiatric symptoms, challenging behavior, or maladjustment. The vast majority of consumers who exhibit challenging behavior or psychiatric symptoms have a green need for acceptance. Many people with green need for acceptance, however, do not have significant psychiatric symptoms.

Possible positive reinforcements include encouragement, acceptance, and praise.

Possible frustrations and, thus, triggers for challenging behavior or psychiatric symptoms include threats to self-concept, such as criticism, put downs, failure, loss of a relationship, rejection, and being yelled at.

At times of behavior crisis, caregivers might be mildly supportive and nonjudgmental. Caregivers should avoid threats, yelling, reprimands, punishment, or criticism. Treatment strategies might include structured experiences or skills training aimed at building self-confidence.

Red Acceptance. People with this need may be self-confident and have positive self-regard. More than their peers, these individuals may be able to deal constructively with criticism, rejection, or failure. Many (not all) give consistent efforts. They are usually in a good mood.

Possible positive reinforcements include opportunities to try new and interesting challenges.

Red Acceptance is associated with mental health and is often a contra-indicator of psychiatric symptoms. Few people with Red Acceptance experience behavioral outbursts or crises.

Need for Attention

This need motivates reactions to the spotlight. People seek attention primarily because it makes them feel important and respected. It is human nature to attend to people who have high status and are respected and, conversely, to ignore those who have low status and are disrespected.

Green Attention. People with this need may behave in ways that draw attention to themselves. Some (not all) may have a habitual tendency to show off and/or want to be treated as special; they may tend to be presumptuous, or to act with a sense of entitlement.

People differ in what it is about themselves they want others to notice and respect. Some call attention to their accomplishments; others to their looks or popularity; and still others call attention to prestigious things they own.

Possible positive reinforcements include adult attention, special activities, rewards, and/or prestigious or expensive material things.

Although many people with Green Attention are mentally healthy, this need sometimes motivates annoying behavior, such as demands to be treated "special,' outrageous behavior, and possibly challenging behavior. When a disorder is present, common diagnoses and symptoms include conduct disorder, personality disorder (dependent, hysterical, or paranoid), paranoia, immature behavior, and in rare cases, self-injurious behavior, Williams syndrome, and Fragile X.

Possible frustrations and, thus, triggers for challenging behavior or psychiatric symptoms include being ignored, nonreinforcement, not being rewarded, and/or caregivers paying attention or making a fuss over someone else. Some (not all) consumers with Green Attention may react suspiciously when they are ignored; they may become confused as to why they are not given the attention/respect they want or think is their due. They may become angry thinking they have been cheated out of their due.

At times of behavior crisis, caregivers might look at pauses during inappropriate outbursts as opportunities to pay positive attention. While ignoring the outburst, called "extinction," may increase a consumer's frustration and irritability, paying attention to it may have the long term effect of reinforcing the challenging behavior. The goal is to find ways to pay attention to the individual's appropriate behavior while ignoring inappropriate behavior.

Red Attention. People with this need are motivated to avoid the limelight. These individuals dislike being noticed, singled out, or treated in special ways. Some (not all) may be motivated toward conventionality so as not to stand out. Some (not all) may be easily embarrassed by attention and, thus, motivated to dress in clothes that do not attract notice.

Attention is a negative reinforcement for these consumers. Some (not all) may be de-motivated by material rewards, especially those that are flashy or noticeable.

The vast majority of people with Red Attention are mentally healthy, but when a disorder is present, they are more likely to exhibit internalizing behaviors, such as sadness, shyness, and anxiety, than attention-grabbing externalizing behaviors.

Possible frustrations and, thus, triggers for challenging behavior or psychiatric symptoms may include attention, being singled out, and embarrassment.

When the individual is upset or in behavior crisis, caregivers might increase the individual's privacy to as great an extent as possible (e.g., ask others to leave the room when their presence isn't necessary for the individual's safety.)

Need for Eating

This need motivates consumption and interest in food.

Green Eating. People with this need tend to have hearty appetites. Green Eaters tend be always thinking about food and may enjoy many different kinds of food, sometimes giving others the impression they would eat almost anything.

Possible reinforcements include opportunities to eat especially favored foods.

Green Eating may be a factor in some eating disorders. Green Eaters may have a tendency to overeat and snack too much, sometimes leading to weight gains or even obesity. Some (not all) may have a tendency to overeat during a stressful period in their lives. Behavioral psychologists, psychiatrists, and nutritionists should be consulted regarding treatment of obesity. People with Prader Willi syndrome tend to have Green Eating.

Possible frustrations and, thus, triggers for challenging behavior or psychiatric symptoms include hunger, delay of meals, poor tasting food, and disliked food.

At times of behavior crisis, Green Eaters may experience hunger or withdrawal of food or hunger as a frustrating experience. On the other hand, consumption of food may temporarily reduce current feelings of frustration.

Red Eating. People with this need tend to have weak appetites. Red Eaters may think about eating only rarely and may be fussy about what they eat.

Although many people with Red Eating are healthy, for some Red Eating may be associated with being underweight. Red Eating also may be associated with certain eating disorders, such as "anorexia nervosa," in which people, usually women, refuse to eat and then lose weight to a point that endangers their health. Behavioral psychologists, psychiatrists, and nutritionists should be consulted regarding treatment of eating disorders. Red Eating also could be a vegetative sign of possible depression.

Possible frustrations and, thus, triggers for challenging behavior or psychiatric symptoms include being pressured to eat too much or disliked foods.

At times of behavior crisis, these individual should not be given food as a reinforcement for positive behavior, or as an incentive to calm down, unless they specifically request it

Need to Help Others

This need motivates the consumer's level of interest regarding the well being of strangers. This need is moderately correlated with intrinsic interest in behaving morally and, to a lesser extent, with intrinsic interest in spending time with one's own family.

Green Helps Others. People with this need may take pride in their responsible and compassionate nature and may intrinsically value altruism.

Possible positive reinforcements include nurturing roles, opportunities to assist others in need, nurturing animals, doll play, visit from family (or extra time with them), and parenting children.

Green Helps Others motivates mostly mentally healthy behaviors and is not diagnostic of a psychiatric disorder. People with this need can be motivated to control their anger/temper for fear of hurting others. For some, this need could signal an increased likelihood of experiencing guilt.

Possible frustrations and, thus, triggers for emotional distress are perceived unfairness, injustice, and outrage. These individuals may become especially bothered watching the suffering or hurt of others.

At times of crisis, caregivers might appeal to the individual's sense of fairness or morals. They might say something like, "You are not behaving the way a good person behaves."

Red Helps Others. People with this need tend to look the other way when another person is hurt or suffering. Some (not all) may feel burdened when taking care of someone in need. Some (not all) may have little interest in family life, especially nurturing roles. Some (not all) may experience visits from members of their family as burdensome.

Although the vast majority of people with Red Helps Others are mentally healthy, some (not all) are at greater risk of challenging behavior, conduct problems, or antisocial behavior. Some (not all) consumers with Red Helps Others may lack compassion and, when provoked, they may not inhibit or moderate any aggressive or antisocial tendencies. Other consumers, such as people with autism, may experience compassion but be inattentive to peers.

At times of behavior crisis, caregivers might call attention to the individual's self-interest and avoid appealing to the individual's sense of fairness or morals. Instead of saying something like, "You are not behaving the way a good person behaves," the caregiver should say something like, "If you calm down, I will play a game with you this evening."

Need for Independence

This need motivates reactions to needing assistance from others and is moderately correlated with interest in leadership roles (psychological trait of "dominance").

Green Independence. People with this need value self-reliance and may not feel comfortable having to rely on others to meet their needs. They may especially dislike when others make decisions on their behalf. They may take pride in having the competencies and resources needed to take care of themselves. Some (not all) may be reluctant to acknowledge their need for others, even to the point where they are reluctant to ask for assistance and may have difficulty expressing gratitude or saying "thank you."

Possible positive reinforcements include opportunities to self-determine one's own life. Some (not all) may enjoy doing things without assistance even though it may take more time or be more difficult. Some (not all) may enjoy leadership roles.

Many people with Green Independence are mentally healthy, although some may be stubborn (display a "my way or the highway" attitude) and may resist going along, to get along. Over a period of time, they gain reputations for being difficult. Some stubborn people may develop adjustment problems or possibly personality disorder.

Possible frustrations and, thus, triggers for challenging behavior or psychiatric symptoms include any situation in which the individual is dependent on others. For some (not all), being directed by others, or being made to do things in ways determined by others, may trigger challenging behavior.

At times of behavior crises, these individuals may respond negatively to being told what to do. Some stubborn people may react negatively to sympathy and closeness, viewing these as intrusions on their independence and ability to do things for themselves. Caregivers may need patience in dealing with these people and may need to provide them with a little more space to calm down on their own (providing of course that their behavior poses no danger to self or others). Some people with Green Independence might benefit from social skills training.

Red Independence. People with this need value support, guidance, or assistance. These individuals may derive comfort knowing they can rely on others in a pinch. People with Red Independence tend to show appreciation when helped. Some (not all) prefer to follow rather than lead. Some (not all) want to feel emotionally close to others, especially those on whom they rely on to meet their needs. Some (not all) may be quick to develop a close relationship with a caregiver. For some the experience – or even the idea – of being on one's own may be frightening.

Possible positive reinforcements include sympathy, support, or warmth from others.

Although many people with Red Independence are mentally healthy, for some (not all) Red Independence may motivate "needy" behavior. Over time, caregivers may feel burdened by frequent requests for assistance. Some highly dependent people are quick to form close relationships, but are devastated when relationships are lost. Psychiatric diagnoses may include dependent personality disorder, adjustment disorder, depression, or anxiety disorder.

Possible frustrations and, thus, triggers for challenging behavior include loss of support, loss of relationships, and being on one's own. When a caregiver leaves his/her job, for example, the dependent individual could have difficulty adjusting to the loss and react with protest behaviors including outbursts of challenging behaviors.

At times of behavior crisis, these individuals may respond best to empathy, assistance, and guidance. They may experience frustration when asked to make frequent decisions or when they are left to meet their own needs without supports.

Need for Learning

This need motivates intellectual activity.

Green Learning. People with this need may enjoy school and formal learning experiences. Some (not all) may like to learn about many different topics or places. These consumers may be easily bored and may have difficulty tolerating boredom. Some (not all) may resent caregivers who treat them as stupid.

Possible positive reinforcements include formal learning experiences and caregivers listening and taking time to explain things.

Green Learning motivates mentally healthy behaviors and is not diagnostic of a psychiatric disorder.

A possible frustrating experience and, thus, trigger for challenging behavior and psychiatric symptoms is boredom.

At times of crisis, talking or listening may help some (not all) people with Green Learning calm down.

Red Learning. People with this need avoid intellectual activities and may be easily frustrated when in school situations. They may especially dislike learning anything they perceive to be irrelevant to their immediate life. At the same time they may rarely ask questions aimed at gaining an understanding of their environment. They may dislike conversations and people who talk a lot.

Possible positive reinforcements include hands on (practical) activities. In school situations, these individuals may need frequent breaks. Learning tasks should be broken down into small, digestible steps. Cessation of learning tasks, conversations, or activities requiring thinking may serve as negative reinforcements.

Although the majority of people with Red Learning are mentally healthy, they are more likely to exhibit learning problems in school, especially low grades and underachievement. Red curiosity is sometimes associated with Attention Deficit Hyperactivity Disorder (ADHD).

Possible frustrations and, thus, triggers for challenging behavior or psychiatric symptoms are encouraged or forced intellectual stimulation such as conversation.

At times of behavior crisis, these individuals may respond best to simple, behavioral instructions as to what they need to do. Too much talking or explaining may irritate them.

Need for Order

This need motivates reactions to orderliness and is highly correlated with reactions to cleanliness.

Green Order. People with this need may embrace organizing behaviors and attention to details.

Positive reinforcements may include cleanliness, routine, preparation, and anything that enhances stability.

Green Order motivates mostly mentally healthy behaviors, but is sometimes associated with autism spectrum disorders, Obsessive-Compulsive Disorder (OCD), or adjustment problems. Some people with Green Order may present with compulsive behaviors. As discussed in Chapter 6, these are repetitive behaviors that are not pleasurable and are thought to reduce or prevent anxiety.

Possible frustrations and, thus, triggers for challenging behavior or psychiatric symptoms include change, especially change in environment or daily routine; interruption or interference with routines; and unpreparedness or ambiguity.

At times of behavior crisis caregivers should not attempt to interrupt ritualistic or compulsive behavior except when such is necessary for the individual's safety. Providing a favored security object (doll, blanket, ball, and chain) may help calm the individual. When these individuals move to another residence, caregivers should maximize the number of familiar activities and objects in the individual's new environment.

Red Order. People with this need may enjoy spontaneity and flexibility. Some (not all) may have a high tolerance for ambiguity and unpredictability. They may tend to overlook details and may be sloppy. Some (not all) may try a new task before finishing the last one.

Positive reinforcements may include opportunities to vary daily schedule or activities or to make things up as the person goes along.

Although Red Order usually motivates mentally healthy behaviors, this need is sometimes associated with underachievement and with regressive behavior. Further, some people with Attention Deficit Hyperactivity Disorder (ADHD) may have Red Order.

Possible frustrations and, thus, triggers for challenging behavior or psychiatric symptoms include rigidly imposed or enforced rules, a high degree of structure, unvaried routines, and/or extensive preparation.

At times of behavior crisis, these individuals may become very sloppy, very messy, or disorganized. Demands for neatness or imposing structure may only frustrate them further. Caregivers may wish to tolerate some messiness at least until the individual calms down.

Need for Physical Activity

This need motivates physical exertion (muscle exercise).

Green Physical Activity. People with this need embrace an active lifestyles and may value fitness, vitality, stamina, and possibly strength.

Possible positive reinforcements include opportunities to play ball, hike, or otherwise engage in physical activities.

Green Physical Activity usually motivates mentally healthy behavior, although in rare instances Green Physical Activity could be associated with overactivity.

Possible frustrations and, thus, triggers for challenging behavior or psychiatric symptoms include restlessness, a lack of opportunity for physical exercise, and inactivity.

At times of behavior crisis, these individuals may display impressive physical endurance.

Red Physical Activity. People with this need have a tendency to be inactive. Some (not all) may be physically lazy to the point of being unfit.

A possible positive reinforcement is the opportunity to rest.

Although Red Physical Activity usually motivates mentally healthy behavior, this need is sometimes associated with obesity. People with Prader Willi syndrome have Red Physical Activity.

Possible frustrations and, thus, triggers for psychiatric symptoms or challenging behavior include demands for physical endurance, exertion, or exercise.

At times of behavior crisis, these individuals could quickly exhaust themselves. Treatment of obesity is best left to behavioral specialists working with nutritionists.

Need for Romance

This need motivates sexual activity and is moderately correlated with appreciation of beauty.

Green Romance. People with this need tend to have above-average interest in sexual experiences. More than their peers, these individuals often may think about sex and may be attracted to many potential partners. Many (not all) may pay attention to their physical attractiveness, that is, their "sex appeal."

Possible positive reinforcements include opportunities for romance such as dating, sexual gratification, and opportunities to improve appearance such as nice clothes.

Although Green Romance usually motivates mentally healthy behavior, it can be a factor in sexual paraphilias, which are indicated by a strong preference for socially disproved means of sexual gratification. Sexual paraphilias include pedophilia (sexual attraction to children); fetishism (the habitual use of a part of the body or an inanimate object to produce sexual gratification); cross-dressing, exhibitionism ("indecent exposure"); frotteurism (obtaining sexual gratification primarily by rubbing and touching against a non consenting person); voyeurism (obtaining sexual gratification primarily by observing nudes or others engage in sexual activity); sadism (obtaining sexual gratification primarily by inflicting pain and humiliation on others); masochism (obtaining sexual gratification primarily by receiving pain); and incest (sexual relationships with a member of one's immediate family.)

Possible frustrations and, thus, triggers for challenging behavior and psychiatric symptoms include sexual deprivation.

Because of the intensity of sexual motivation, sexually inappropriate behavior can be very difficult to manage. Treatment is best conducted by behavioral experts specializing in sexual problems.

Red Romance. People with this need tend to have below-average interest in sexual experiences. They may spend little time thinking about and pursuing sex. Many (not all) may pay minimal attention to their physical attractiveness ("sex appeal"). They may occasionally enjoy sex, but have little interest in frequent sex.

Some (not all) people with Red Romance dislike sex. They may have been taught puritanical attitudes and, thus, may become anxious in sexual situations. They may have doubts about their sexual skills. They may have had unpleasant experiences with sex when they were younger. Some (not all) may find some aspects of sex disgusting.

Although Red Romance usually motivates mentally healthy behavior, this need could be a sign of fear of poor performance or guilt related to sexual experience. Red Romance also could result from any of a number of health issues, such as diabetes. An abrupt loss of sexual interest is sometimes indicative of unhappiness or depression.

Possible frustrations and, thus, triggers for challenging behavior and psychiatric symptoms include expectations of sexual performance, sexualized stimuli, and observations of nudity.

Sexually inappropriate behavior can be very difficult to manage. Treatment is best conducted by behavioral experts specializing in sexual problems.

Need for Social Contact

This need motivates reactions to social opportunities with peers.

Green Social Contact. People with this need tend to be gregariousness. They may value social skills that attract others and keep friends. Some (not all) may show above-average interest in fooling around and having fun.

Possible positive reinforcements include opportunities to socialize, attend parties, have fun, and play with friends.

Green Social Contact motivates mostly mentally healthy behaviors and is not diagnostic of any psychiatric disorder.

Possible frustrations and, thus, triggers for challenging behavior and psychiatric symptoms include social isolation and solitude.

At times of behavior crisis, these individuals might be calmed by the presence of peers.

Red Social Contact. People with this need spend a lot of time alone in solitude. These individuals may value having a few close friends rather than many superficial friends. Some (not all) are quiet and serious. People with Red Social Contact may have poor social skills, because of a lack of interest in socializing rather than a lack of social learning opportunities. Some show little interest in peers.

Possible positive reinforcements include opportunities for quiet time, privacy, and solitude.

Although Red Social Contact motivates mostly mentally healthy behavior, in some instances Red Social Contact could be an indicator of depression, avoidant symptoms, autism, Prader Willi syndrome, or withdrawal

Possible frustrations and, thus, triggers for challenging behavior and psychiatric symptoms include prolonged social interactions and perhaps practical jokes or fooling around. Social experiences may drain the energy of some people with Red Social Contact.

At times of crisis, the presence of peers or demands to socialize may add to a consumer's frustration, whereas quiet time alone may have a calming effect.

Need for Tranquility

This need motivates reactions to physical danger and is broken down into two correlated components, called anxiety sensitivity and pain sensitivity.

Green Tranquility. People with this need tend to be fearful, nervous, stressed, and worriers. They may handle stress poorly and/or become easily frightened. Many (not all) have little tolerance for physical pain.

Possible positive reinforcements include opportunities to relax, staying close to home, companionship, and familiar places, objects, or people.

Although Green Tranquility usually motivates normal timidity, sometimes this need may indicate risk for anxiety disorder. People with Green Tranquility may be at risk for post-traumatic stress disorder, phobia, and panic disorder. People with this need are also at increased risk for substance abuse, especially alcoholism. People with autism, and some people with self-injurious behavior, may have Green Tranquility.

Because Green Tranquility is correlated with low tolerance for physical pain, some consumers may be quick to complain about stomachaches, headaches, or other aches and pains. Sometimes these complaints indicate somatoform disorder.

Possible frustrations and, thus, triggers for challenging behavior and psychiatric symptoms include dares, danger, excitement, pain, injury, loud sounds, sudden changes in environment, and travel away from where one lives.

At times of behavior crisis caregivers should avoid doing anything that might further frighten the individual or contribute to his/her stress. Instead, caregivers should attempt to remove feared or anxiety-eliciting stimuli and speak in a soothing voice that is stress free and not loud. Familiar people or objects may reduce the consumer's anxiety. Consideration should be given to the possibility that the individual is in pain.

Desensitization/ exposure therapies are first line treatments for fears. These treatments are best attempted by behavior therapists with expertise in anxiety disorders.

Red Tranquility. People with this need tend to be courageous, fearless, and/or somewhat insensitive to pain.

Possible positive reinforcements include adventures, travel, thrills, and excitement.

Red Tranquility motivates mostly mentally healthy behavior. In a small percentage of people, however, Red Tranquility motivates excessive risk-taking or recklessness. Red Tranquility is more likely to be associated with externalizing than with internalizing behavior.

Possible frustrations and, thus, triggers for challenging behavior and psychiatric symptoms include a daily schedule that lacks adventure and is viewed by the individual as boringly safe and lacking in adventure.

Red Tranquility motivates tolerance of physical pain. People with this need might not complain about stomachaches, headaches, and minor bodily pains.

At times of behavior crisis these individuals might not respond to threats, pain, or danger.

Need for Vengeance

This need motivates an individual's reactions to provocation.

Green Vengeance. People with this need may embrace confrontation and competitive behavior. Some (not all) are aggressive and may enjoy confrontation so much they go looking for trouble. They may admire fighters and may disrespect people who back down from confrontation.

Possible positive reinforcements include winning, competitive games, debating, and/or protecting.

Many people with Green Vengeance are mentally health individuals who enjoy competition. Some (not all) may cope poorly with anger, frustration, and/or irritability. They may struggle to control their tempers and may be combative. Many (not all) hold grudges. Green Vengeance sometimes motivates inappropriate aggression, anger management problems, oppositional behavior, and challenging behavior.

Possible frustrations and, thus, triggers for challenging behavior and psychiatric symptoms include the primal provocations. These are as follows: delay; having something taken away; loss/treat to status (e.g., loss of attention, possessions, or privileges); threats to territory (e.g., invasion of personal space); competition for resources; restricted access to potential mates; strange or unfamiliar people; aggressive or unfriendly displays by other people; interruptions or delays in consumption of reinforcements (e.g., taking away food, interruption sex).

At times of behavior crisis these individual may become frustrated, irritable, destructive, brutal, and violent. Provocations should be minimized. Loud noises should be kept to a minimum. Caregivers should remain calm even when the individual attempts to provoke them.

Some people with Green Vengeance might benefit from professionally taught anger management training.

Red Vengeance. People with this need may avoid conflict and embrace cooperative behavior even when they are provoked. Often their first impulse is to cooperate rather than compete. These individuals are peace-keepers.

Possible positive reinforcements include reconciliation behaviors that signal the end of a conflict and serve to reduce future conflict. The primal reconciliation behaviors include submissive displays, sharing, cooperative play, apologies, holding hands, and kissing.

Although Red Vengeance usually motivates mentally healthy behavior, this need is sometimes associated with symptoms of internalizing disorders such as nonassertive behavior, not fighting back when others take advantage, or passive aggression. Caregivers may find they need to protect these gentle individuals from possible abuse by others.

Possible frustrations and, thus, triggers for challenging behavior and psychiatric symptoms include threats, aggression, confrontation, violence, and anger shown by others.

At times of behavior crisis, these individuals may respond best to kindness and gentleness and poorly to anger or provocation.

Conclusion

We have considered numerous practical suggestions regarding how knowledge of a person's green and red needs may identify:

> possible triggers for the challenging behavior and psychiatric symptoms the individual may have;

> possible positive reinforcements for the individual;

> possible diagnostic conditions.

At most the information in this chapter has only statistical validity for which there could be many individual exceptions. All of the suggestions in this chapter, therefore, need to be verified for each individual consumer, and none should be applied automatically as if they were universal and absolute truisms, which they are not. It is believed, however, that by focusing on each individual's unique needs, rather than on generic diagnoses, a much wider range of possible frustrating experiences and positive reinforcements will be considered when supervising and caring for people with a dual diagnosis.

Chapter 10

Motivation in Schools

N ow that we have seen how human needs play out in dual diagnosis, we turn our attention to increasing positive outcomes in schools. Historically, two groups have studied motivation among students with ID.

Edward Zigler and his colleagues studied five motives in detail: dependency, fear of strangers, expectancy of success, outerdirectedness, and competence motivation (Zigler, Bennet-Givens, & Hodapp 1999). This work encouraged attention to the needs of the "whole person" at a time when the ID field was narrowly focused on the trait of sub-average intelligence. Zigler was an extraordinarily productive researcher and an effective advocate for the developmental model of research. His effort to broaden how we think about intellectual disabilities has had significant influence.

Carl Haywood and his students studied intrinsic motivation (Switzkey, 1999). This work represented an effort to improve the education of people with ID. Intrinsic motivation theory, however, had only limited influence in the ID field, which historically was more interested in behaviorist models of education.

In this chapter the 16 human needs are applied to issues relevant to schools, especially achievement motivation and curiosity. We will consider the following three hypotheses:

Hypothesis I. The distinction between intrinsic and extrinsic motivation is invalid.

Hypothesis II. Intellectual and exploratory curiosities constitute two distinct, largely unrelated motives.

Hypothesis III. Achievement motivation can be broken down into at least six distinguishable components, each with different implications for intervention.

These three hypotheses apply to students with and without ID. They are most relevant to students aged 12 and up (junior high, senior high, and college). The best work in assessing psychological needs in children under the age of 12 has been reported by Zigler and his colleagues (Zigler, Bennet-Givens, & Hodapp 1999).

Hypothesis I: Intrinsic And Extrinsic Motivation

Deci (1975) and Deci and Ryan (1985) distinguished between intrinsic and extrinsic goals. Intrinsic goals are valued for their own sake, whereas extrinsic goals are valued only because they produce intrinsic goals. Table 10-1 shows how 12 human needs divide into intrinsic versus extrinsic categories.

Table 10.1 Extrinsic versus Intrinsic Human Needs

Extrinsic Motives	Intrinsic Motives
Eating	Learning
Tranquility	Social Contact
Romance	Physical activity
Vengeance	Independence
Attention	Helps Others
	Acceptance
	Order

The theory of intrinsic and extrinsic motivation has significant similarities with Plato's (1966/360 BCE) philosophy of mind-body dualism. Where Plato distinguished between mind versus body; Deci (1975) distinguishes between the Central Nevous System and tissue needs. Plato's mental motives (e.g., Learning and Social Contact) are intrinsic motives for Deci and Ryan (1985), whereas Plato's body motives (such as Romance and Eating) are extrinsic motives for Deci and Ryan. Just as Plato suggested that the motives of the mind are superior to those of the body, Deci and Ryan held that intrinsic motivation is superior to extrinsic motivation. Where Plato held that the motives of the body contaminate those of the mind (e.g., sexual desire interferes with Learning), Deci and Ryan (1985) held that extrinsic motives undermine intrinsic motives.

The central scientific issue regarding intrinsic/extrinsic motivation is to justify the classification of motives. Are the Table 10-1 dualistic categories scientifically valid? Why are the needs for eating, tranquility, romance, vengeance, and attention considered to be examples of extrinsic motives? Why are the needs for learning, social contact, physical activity, independence, helps others, acceptance, and order considered to be examples of intrinsic motives? What, if anything, justifies this dualistic classification of psychological needs?

Theorists have given at least four different definitions of the distinction between intrinsic and extrinsic motivation. Each definition asserts certain qualities argued to be true of all intrinsic motives but of no extrinsic motives. We will consider each of these definitions.

Competence Definition. Some theorists have held that intrinsic motives are engaged in for the purpose of feeling competent (Deci & Ryan, 1985; Switzky, 1999; White, 1959). Regarding Table 10-1, this view implies that needs for learning, social contact, physical activity, independence, and helps others produce feelings of competence, but needs for eating, tranquility, romance, vengeance, and attention do not produce feelings of competence.

I believe this view is simply untrue. Competence does not validly distinguish between intrinsic and extrinsic motives. Extrinsic motives could be about competence, same as intrinsic motives. Winning, for example, sometimes leads to feelings of competence, but competition (which falls under vengeance) is regarded as an extrinsic motive. Since the extrinsic motive of competition could lead to feelings of competence, competence is not a valid basis for classifying motives into the intrinsic/extrinsic categories shown in Table 1.

Even the originator of competence motivation theory was skeptical about its validity. White (1959) wrote, "No doubt it will at first seem arbitrary to propose a single motivational conception in connection with so many diverse kinds of behavior. What do we gain by attributing motivational unity to such a diverse array of activities?" (p. 317). I agree with White's skepticism that intrinsic motives are too diverse to be about the single goal of competence.

Internal-External Definition. Deci (1975) and Deci and Ryan (1985) held that extrinsic motives are instigated by environmental factors, whereas intrinsic motives are instigated by factors within the central nervous system. They claimed that deprivation of "tissue needs" instigate extrinsic motives (such as hunger) but not intrinsic motives (such as loneliness). As far as I could discern, they presented no neuropsychological evidence to support this distinction.

However, the idea that one part of anatomy supports extrinsic motivation, whereas a different part supports intrinsic motivation, is outdated speculation. It is not true that environmental deprivation instigates extrinsic motives but not intrinsic motives. A lack of stimulus novelty, for example, will arouse curiosity, just as enslavement will strengthen the motive for freedom. In these simple examples we see how environmental deprivation (sameness, enslavement) can instigate the intrinsic motives of learning and independence. Again, we see that motives are far too diverse to be reduced to a physiological version of mind (central nervous system) versus body (tissue needs).

Hedonism. Weiner (1995) suggested that intrinsic motivation is an inherently enjoyable behavior, whereas extrinsic motivation is something else. This view, however, exaggerates the role of pleasure in human motivation.

Pleasure theories have difficulty explaining how intrinsic motives temporarily satiate. All intrinsic motives turn on and off: Sometimes we are motivated to explore; after a period of time exploring, we lose interest and want to do something else; and after a period to time of not exploring, we again become motivated to explore. If exploring were inherently pleasurable, why would we ever tire of it and move on to find pleasure doing something else? People value pleasure even more when they are tired than when they are rested; the desire for pleasure does not satiate, but intrinsic motives do.

Historically, pleasure theory was based on a formal error in logic called the error of consequence. The fact that pleasure is a consequence of getting what we want does not mean that pleasure is what we wanted in the first place. A scholar might read a book in order to learn, which might be pleasurable, but the scholar's aim was knowledge, not pleasure. Hedonists have exaggerated the motivational implications of pleasure in human behavior.

Means-Ends. Deci (1975) likened intrinsic motivation to Aristotelian ends, and extrinsic motivation to Aristotelian means. Ends are what people want, whereas means are methods for getting what we want. Eating a steak, for example, is a means of gratifying our need for food, which is an end.

An Aristotelian means-ends analysis does not justify social psychology's distinction between intrinsic and extrinsic motives. In Table 10-1 each so-called intrinsic motive is a mean or an end depending on the individual's goal. A person might learn, for example, either because he/she intrinsically values knowledge, or because he/she can instrumentally use knowledge to get promoted at work. Whether each so-called extrinsic motive is a mean or an end depends on the goal. A person might eat, for example, because he/she is hungry (eating as an end) or because he/she does not wish to insult the cook (eating as an instrumental goal).

If an extrinsic reward did not produce an intrinsically valued stimulus, the extrinsic reward would lack motivational properties. Aristotelian means are motivational only because they are connected to ends; without ends, there could be no instrumental (extrinsic) motivation.

Conclusion. Similar to how Plato divided motives into mind versus body – a theory called philosophical dualism – Deci (1975) and Deci and Ryan (1985) divided human goals into intrinsic and extrinsic motives. They say that needs such as learning and physical activity are categorically different from needs such as eating and romance. But there is no direct evidence of construct validity for this dualistic classification of human motives. Intrinsic motivation theorists have offered four different analyses aimed at justifying their dualistic classification of motives, but all four are flawed. Goals cannot be classified into just two kinds, internal vs. external, pleasurable vs. non-pleasurable, etc. Instead, there are many different kinds of goals. Reiss (2008) has summarized evidence from cross-cultural studies with thousands of people validating 16 human needs, each of which motivates different intrinsically valued goals. This scientifically valid research suggested there are 16 kinds of motives, not two, and all are intrinsic motives.

So, as stated in Hypothesis I, the distinction between intrinsic and extrinsic motivation is invalid. Extrinsic motivation does not exist; what some have identified as "extrinsic motives" are really methods for gratifying intrinsic motives. Motivation arises from human needs that cannot be divided into just two types, whether based on competence, causes, pleasure, nor function.

Hypothesis II: Two Kinds of Curiosity

You have heard the myth. Babies are born with natural curiosity; they scan and roam their environments. Young children start school so eager to learn they are wide eyed and thrilled. Rather than nurture this natural curiosity, teachers unwittingly turn the fun of learning into a rat race for good grades and academic awards. They even subject students to high-stake tests. In no time at all, the schools have extinguished the natural curiosity out of their students. The students now hate school and lack motivation.

As Kohn (1993) asserted,

> All of us start out in life intensely fascinated by the world around us and inclined to explore it without any extrinsic inducement.... Most American schools marinate students in behaviorism, so the result, unsurprisingly, is that children's intrinsic motivation drains away. They typically become more and more extrinsically oriented as they get older and progress through elementary school (p. 91).

This myth is right on two counts; babies enjoy exploring their environments, and many middle and high school students dislike school. The error is in assuming that the exploratory behavior of babies has something to do with the intellectual behavior of adolescents.

Intrinsic motivation theory says that exploratory behavior and intellectual activity are two variants of an underlying interest in learning (about new stimuli). People like to explore novel situations, and they like to learn about new places.

Based on my studies of life motives, I suspect intrinsic motivation theory is invalid. Consider the people you know who are explorers. Notice that only some of them are also thinkers. Consider the people you know who are thinkers. Notice that only some of them are also explorers. Intrinsic motivation theory implies that exploring (e.g., babies roaming environments) and thinking (e.g., students learning math) are commonly motivated by a need for stimulus novelty, but this assumption seems to be invalid.

Daniel Boone was a legendary eighteenth century explorer. John Filson described him as a "curious" man because Boone loved to explore new places. Yet Boone also disliked being confined to a room and, thus, hated school. He took to "rough male sports" much more than he took to book learning.

Issac Newton was arguably the most influential intellectual ever. He had a thirst for knowledge even as a young boy. He observed somebody hit a tennis ball and wondered about the paths of projectiles. Although Newton was always thinking, he wasn't much for exploring. He spent many months more or less alone in his Cambridge University dormitory working on exciting new mathematical ideas.

Explorers like Boone aren't necessarily intellectuals like Newton, and intellectuals like Newton aren't necessarily explorers like Boone. We should not assume that exploratory and intellectual behavior is motivated by a common curiosity.

The exploratory behavior of babies does not imply that high school students were born with a natural curiosity for intellectual learning. Exploratory curiosity is quite different from intellectual curiosity. Exploratory curiosity (the attraction of novel stimuli) motivates both babies and adults to scan and roam their environments except when fear of the unknown inhibits exploration. Yet if high school teachers were to stimulate the exploratory curiosity of their students, the students might roam hallways or the local community, but that would not lead to better grades. In terms of Reiss's (2008) taxonomy of 16 life motives, exploratory curiosity is motivated by a combination of self-confidence (which falls under weak need for acceptance) and courage (which falls under a weak need for tranquility).

In contrast, intellectual curiosity motivates people to sustain thinking in the pursuit of knowledge and truth (Cacioppo, Petty, Feinstein, & Jarvis, 1996) and is primarily about abstraction, thinking, and cognition. In terms of Reiss's (2008) 16 life motives, for example, intellectual curiosity falls under a need for cognition (learning) and is largely uncorrelated with exploratory behavior.

Since exploratory and intellectual curiosities are two different motives, coincidentally some people enjoy both exploring and thinking. John Glenn, the first man to walk on the moon, enjoyed science. Edmund Hillary, the first man to explore the peak of Mount Everest, wrote a number of books. The mythical men of the starship Enterprise were scientists; known throughout the universe as a great thinker, Spock boldly went where no man had gone before.

Hypothesis III: Six Motivational Reasons for Underachievement

Hypothesis III is that achievement motivation can be broken down into at least six distinguishable components, each with different implications for intervention (Reiss, 2009). In the remainder of this chapter, I will briefly discuss each of the six components of achievement motivation in terms of how they impact grades in school.

The RMP-ID may be administered to junior or senior high school students to evaluate how they prioritize 12 human needs. In contrast, the RMP (school version) should be used with middle and high school students with IQs in the "borderline" range of IQ (Reiss, & Reiss, 1984). As discussed below, the results of these assessments may identify some of the motivational causes for low grades in schools.

Reason No. 1: Lack of Curiosity (low scores on RMP-ID learning scale). I distinguish between intelligence and intellectual curiosity. Intelligence is an indicator of one's ability to solve problems, whereas intellectual curiosity is an indicator of one's motivation (or need) to think. The two traits are only moderately correlated (Cacioppo et al., 1996). Some people are more intelligent than they are curious, and others are more curious than they are intelligent.

Many students with low grades have only a weak (red) need for learning (Kavanaugh & Reiss, 2001). These students become frustrated when asked to concentrate and sustain their thoughts, whatever the topic, because they lack intellectual curiosity in general, as opposed to a lack of curiosity in particular subjects.

Incurious people simply dislike having to think. As one middle school

113

student wondered, "Why can't they invent a pill I could take when I need to know something?" This student wanted to bypass frustrating learning processes and get right to the valuable result. He wanted to be knowledgeable, but he did not want to think in order to do so.

Intellectual curiosity determines how much a person values theoretical ideas. I know highly curious professors who strongly believe that universities are about intellectual activities, not practical matters, to the extent that they believe universities should offer faculty status to somebody who writes books about Picasso, but not to Picasso himself. In their view, writing books about art is an intellectual activity "worthy" of a university, while creating art is a practical activity better suited to some other venue.

Incurious people have the potential to value knowledge they can put to use. I recall a radio talk show host who criticized a U. S. President for lacking intellectual curiosity, and then said he was baffled by the President's detailed knowledge of politics. How can a President lacking in intellectual curiosity spend many hours studying the precinct-by- precinct results of the last several elections? Answer: because he or she values practical information over abstract thought. Apparently, the radio host did not know that a person can lack intellectual curiosity but still show interest in practical knowledge. A weak need for intellectual curiosity predicts only that the President will not apply himself to the study of theoretical, impractical ideas.

Incurious students may be interested in relevant knowledge but not in theoretical ideas. They might be interested in learning how to fix cars, for example, but not about the "big bang" that gave birth to the universe. They might be interested in learning how to shoot a basketball or make furniture, but not about the inauguration of President James Madison in 1809. They may complain that the school curriculum is boring or irrelevant, but that is because they naturally dislike intellectual activities that require them to learn about anything they cannot put to use in their current life.

People are born with the potential for varying degrees of interest in the intellectual aspects of life. Some students think about things nearly all the time, others not at all. A lack of curiosity is most often the result of normal variations in how long an individual can sustain thinking before becoming frustrated. A lack of curiosity is not necessarily a sign of a disorder.

Although a weak need for learning could explain poor grades, it is not an excuse. These students lack natural motivation for school learning, but they can be motivated to learn with self-discipline, rewards, incentives, and good parenting. Parents should expect intellectually incurious students to graduate from high school, complete their homework assignments on time, and pass their tests.

Students who lack intellectual curiosity will struggle in school, but they may have the potential to excel in other areas of life such as work, family, or sports.

Reason No. 2: Lack of Ambition (low scores on RMP-ID independence scale). Laid-back students, who lack will and initiative, resist trying to influence other people. They are onlookers who prefer to watch events unfold without trying to influence what happens.

Many experts misunderstand laid-back students and think they lack self-confidence and hold back effort out of fear of failure. Actually, a lack of ambition is unrelated to a lack of self-confidence (Reiss, 2008). These students do not lack ambition because they are insecure; they lack ambition because they dislike influencing other people. Some are quite comfortable with the idea that they should not let their schooling or career interfere with their enjoyment of life.

These students underachieve because they do not apply themselves. They set modest goals and avoid challenging courses because they do not want to work hard. Those who are smart still may earn average or even above average grades, but only when they can do so without working hard. Such students may be willing to work at a moderate pace but no harder. While some teachers will dismiss them as "unmotivated" or "lazy," they are actually strongly motivated to avoid hard work. Compared to the average student, laid-back students place higher value on leisure and lower value on achieving. Indeed, when a laid-back student is pushed to work hard, the individual may quit. Teachers and parents need to be careful in how much pressure they place on these students.

Since achievement is not one of their priorities, students who lack ambition may have a tendency to underachieve throughout life. Parents and counselors need to work with these children to set mutually agreed standards for the grades they will earn. These students may want to avoid the most challenging courses, but they can do well in moderately challenging courses. What is "challenging" or "moderately challenging," of course, depends on the student's potential.

Parents and teachers need to be careful not to think something is wrong with students who lack ambition. Nothing is wrong with laid-back students; they just have values different from those of high achievers.

Reason No. 3: Fear of Failure (high scores on RMP-ID acceptance scale.) A number of scholarly papers have linked the fear of failure to underachievement (e.g., Atkinson & Feather, 1966; Hill, 1972). Students afraid to fail worry about their grades and may show test anxiety. They may give inconsistent effort and may tend to procrastinate, putting off homework assignments or not studying for tests until it is too late. Some may give good effort on easy tasks but not when challenged and/or become known for poor effort or for inconsistency of effort.

Students who fear failure respond poorly to criticism, sometimes to the point that they may not hear what a critical teacher or parent is saying. Criticism may cause them to quit or at least perform poorly. Some under-achieving students would improve their grades if their teachers or parents became less critical of them. They need encouragement to give maximum effort and are at their best when parents and teachers stand behind and encourage them. They may respond to teachers who are nonjudgmental and work best in supportive, uncritical environments. They may need self-confidence and should be encouraged to concentrate on their strengths, and not on their weaknesses.

Psychological feelings of insecurity are very common and, in that sense, are normal. A strong need for acceptance (insecurity in the upper 20% of the population), however, is *sometimes* an indicator of a psychological disorder and need for counseling. School psychologists using the RMP have noticed that many students referred to them score high on need for acceptance, indicating a possible lack of self-esteem.

Reason No. 4: Combativeness (high scores on RMP-ID vengeance scale). Some students with high need for vengeance appear to be looking for trouble. They can get themselves into so much trouble it distracts them from their school work, leading to grades significantly below their capability.

Combativeness is an important cause of underachievement throughout life. Combative schoolchildren get into fights on the playground, school cafeteria, school hallways, or even in the classroom itself (Mandel, 1997). Combative adults fight so many battles with others they become distracted from what they need to do to get ahead. They have a tendency to make enemies of potential friends. Boys are more likely to be combative than are girls.

Students with a high need for vengeance are attentive to issues of insult, competition, and conflict. They are quick to take offense and to fight back. They are impressed with peers who win fights and may be much more likely than the average student to be referred to the principal's office for discipline violations (Kavanaugh & Reiss, 2001).

Parents and counselors should help combative students find socially appropriate outlets for their confrontational nature. Many careers reward competitiveness including sports, military life, and business. The student may need to learn the difference between socially appropriate competition versus inappropriate or excessive confrontation or aggression. They may need to be taught the potentially severe damage to reputation or status that can result from inappropriate confrontations and outbursts. Some highly competitive students may benefit from anger management training.

Reason No. 5: Spontaneity (low scores on RMP-ID order scale). Spontaneous people underachieve when they have too many balls in the air. They do not complete what they begin: They tend to start a new task before they finish work on the old task. Their carelessness, sloppiness, and lack of attention to detail also tend to hold them back. Teaching them organization or planning skills is largely unhelpful because they are disorganized by nature, not by a lack of skills. Since they value their ability to adjust to events as they arise, they have little use for plans.

These students need to be taught to complete one task before moving on to the next. They also may need to learn how others perceive them. Some spontaneous students think they are impressing teachers by working on multiple projects, when in reality the teachers are thinking they are too scattered to do any one job well. Counselors should directly bring these misperceptions to the attention of spontaneous students as part of their effort to encourage them to manage their spontaneity for a greater level of achievement.

Reason No. 6: Expedience (low scores on the RMP-ID helps others scale). Expedient students can be disloyal, irresponsible, and untrustworthy. They underachieve when they shirk their homework and other school responsibilities. Some teachers mark them down for being irresponsible or lacking in character.

These students need to learn that their teachers and parents are not going to let them get away with anything. They need to be taught that people who cheat are very likely to get caught eventually. They may need teachers and family to impose strict ethical limits. They will play by the rules only when it is to their advantage to do so.

Conclusion

The ideas presented in this chapter differ significantly from traditional thinking about how students learn in school. Dualism, including intrinsic and extrinsic motivation, is rejected in favor of the view that 16 human needs motivate behavior. Further, exploratory curiosity and intellectual curiosity are distinguished; exploratory curiosity involves novel stimuli arousing interest but also the fear of the unknown, while intellectual curiosity is a need for cognition. Together, these ideas imply that teachers cannot tap into the "natural curiosity" of some of their students, but instead must rely on incentives, such as grades and gold stars, to motivate students with subaverage curiosity.

We should not think of students with poor grades in school as unmotivated, but rather as motivated in directions other than academic pursuits. This chapter delineates six motivational reasons for poor grades in school: lack of intellectual curiosity, lack of ambition, fear of failure, combativeness, spontaneity, and expedience. School psychologists can use the RMP and RMP-ID assessment tools to assess which of these six motives apply to any individual middle or high school student with or without ID.

Appendix A

Glossary of Certain Terms Used in This Book

Acceptance	Need for acceptance motivates how individual reacts to criticism and failure.
Attention	Need for attention motivates how individual reacts to the spotlight.
Average need	Term is applied when the strength of an individual's need is in the middle 60% the population. Term is used interchangeably with "Yellow need."
Basic desire	A universal motive that can be satiated only temporarily and, thus, influences behavior over the lifespan. Term is used interchangeably with terms "human need" and "life motive."
Challenging behavior	A severe and chronic behavior problem not easily diagnosed as a mental illness or personality disorder. Same as "severe behavior disorder."
Consumer	Any individual with ID in need of services.
Crisis intervention	Any effort intended to calm down an individual with ID who is very upset and possibly exhibiting challenging behavior.
Diagnostic overshadowing	The tendency for mental health disorders to seem less significant than they really are when considered in the context of ID.
DSM	Widely-used acronym for the official nomenclature of the American Psychiatric Association.
Eating	Need for eating motivates the individual's habitual appetite.
Exploratory curiosity	The attraction of novel stimuli; novel stimuli arouses interest but also fear of the unknown.
Feel-good happiness	Sensual pleasure; positive sensations.

Green need	Term is applied when the strength of an individual's need is in the upper 20% of the population. Term is used interchangeably with "strong need" and "high need."
Helps others	Motivates concern about the well being of others.
High need	Term is applied when the strength of an individual's need is in the upper 20% of the population. Term is used interchangeably with "green need" and "strong need."
Human need	A universal motive that can be satiated only temporarily and, thus, influences behavior over the lifespan. Term is used interchangeably with terms "life motive" and "basic desire."
Intellectual curiosity	The need for cognition, which motivates intellectual activity (thinking).
Independence	This need motivates reactions to assistance from others.
ID	Intellectual disabilities (formerly, mental retardation).
Learning	This need motivates intellectual activity.
Life motive	A universal motive that can be satiated only temporarily and, thus, influences behavior over the lifespan. Term is used interchangeably with terms "human need" and "basic desire."
Low need	Term is applied when the strength of an individual's need is in the bottom 20% of the population. Term is used interchangeably with "weak need" and "Red need."
Mental illness	A mental health disorder that is coded on Axis I in DSM. In this book, the term refers primarily to those mental health disorders with regressive onsets.
NADD	Current name, and former acronym, of the National Association for the Dually Diagnosed.

Order	This need motivates reactions to orderliness and cleanliness.
Person-Centered Planning	Various efforts to plan lifestyles and daily schedules for people with ID, giving emphasis to the individual's own aspirations, goals, and dreams.
PCP	Acronym for person-centered planning.
Personality disorder	A mental health disorder that is coded on Axis II in DSM. In this book, the term refers primarily to those disorders with gradual onsets (that is, little or no regression.)
Priority of need	The strength of a need for a particular individual; that is, whether a need is green, yellow, or red.
Quality of life	Individual's global satisfaction with main areas of life such as independence, residence, work, social life, family life, and access to the community.
Red need	Term is applied when the strength of an individual's need is in the bottom 20% of the population. Term is used interchangeably with "weak need" and "low need."
Reiss Motivation Profile	A standardized psychological assessment of human needs. Some versions are questionnaires; others are rating scales. Some versions are used with the general public; other versions (RMP-MRDD and the newer RMP ID) are used with people with intellectual disabilities.
Reiss Screens	Two caretaker rating scales used to assess the need for further evaluation for possible dual diagnosis. The 38-item Reiss Screen is used with people with ID age 16 or higher, and the 60-item Reiss Scales are used with people with ID between the ages of 4 and 21.
Severe behavior disorder	A significant and chronic behavior problem not easily diagnosed as a mental illness or personality disorder. Same as "challenging behavior."

Strong need	Term is applied when the strength of an individual's need is in the upper 20% of the population. Term is used interchangeably with "Green need" and "high need."
Value-based happiness	A general sense that one's life has purpose and meaning.
Weak need	Term is applied when the strength of an individual's need is in the bottom 20% of the population. Term is used interchangeably with "Red need" and "low need".
Yellow need	Term is applied when the strength of an individual's need is in the middle 60% the population. Term is used interchangeably with "average need".

Appendix B

References

Abraham, K. (1911). Notes on the psychoanalytic investigation and treatment of manic-depressive insanity and allied conditions. *Selected Papers on Psychoanalysis.* New York: Basic Books.

Amabile, T.M., Hill, K. G., Hennessey, B. A., & Tighe, E. M. (1994). The work preference inventory: Assessing intrinsic and extrinsic motivational orientations. *Journal of Personality and Social Psychology, 66,* 950-967.

Aman, M. G., Singh, N. N., Stewart, A. W., & Field, C. J. (1985). The Aberrant Behavior Checklist manual: A behavior rating scale for the assessment of treatment effects. *American Journal of Mental Deficiency, 89,* 485-491.

Aristotle (1953). *The Nichomachean ethics* (trans. J. A. K. Thompson). New York: Penguin Books. (Original work created about 330 B.C.E.).

Asmundson, G. (1999). Anxiety sensitivity and chronic pain: Empirical findings, clinical implications, and future directors. In S. Taylor (ed.), *Anxiety sensitivity: Theory research, and treatment of the fear of anxiety* (pp. 269-285). Mahwah, NJ: Lawrence Erlbaum.

Asmundson, G., & Taylor, S. (1996). Role of anxiety sensitivity in pain-related fear and avoidance. *Journal of Behavioral Medicine, 19,* 577-586.

Atkinson, J. W., & Feather, N. T. (1966). *A theory of achievement motivation.* New York: Wiley.

Aureli, F., & de Waal, F. B. M. (2000). *Natural conflict resolution.* Berkeley: University of California Press.

Baker, B. L., Blacher, J., & Pfeiffer, S. (1993). Family involvement in residential treatment of children with psychiatric disorder and mental retardation. *Hospital and Community Psychiatry, 44,* 561-566.

Bandura, A. (1977). *Social learning theory.* Englewood Cliffs, NJ: Prentice-Cliffs.

Bandura, A., & Walters, R. H. (1963). *Social learning and personality development*. New York: Holt.

Barnett, P. A., & Gotlib, I. H. (1988). Psychosocial functioning and depression: Distinguishing among antecedents, concomitants, and consequences. *Psychological Bulletin, 104*, 97-126.

Batchelor, I. R. C. (1964). The diagnosis of schizophrenia. *Proceedings of the Royal Society of Medicine, 57*, 417-419.

Beasley, A., & Rowell, K. (2003). Differences in motivations between fundamental Christians and atheists on the Reiss Profile of Fundamental Goals and Motivational Sensitivities. *Education Resources Information Center* (ED479165).

Benson, B. A. (1990). Anger management training. In A. Dosen, A. Van Gennep, & G. Zwanikken (Eds.), *Proceedings of the International Congress on the Treatment of Mental Illness and Behavioural Disorders in the Mentally Retarded*. Leiden, Holland: PAOS.

Benson, B. A. (1985). Behavior disorders and mental retardation: Associations with age, sex, and level of functioning in an outpatient clinic sample. *Applied Research in Mental Retardation, 6*, 79-85.

Benson, B. A., & Ivins, J. (1992). Anger, depression, and self-concept in adults with mental retardation. *Journal of Intellectual Disability Research, 36*, 169-175.

Benson, B. A., & Laman, D. S. (1988). Suicidal tendencies of mentally retarded adults in community settings. *Australia and New Zealand Journal of Developmental Disabilities, 14*, 49- 54.

Benson, B.A., Reiss, S., Smith, D.C., & Laman, D.C. (1985). Psychosocial correlates of depression in mentally retarded adults II: Poor social skills. *American Journal of Mental Deficiency, 89*, 657-659.

Berkson, G., & Romer, D. (1980a). Social ecology of supervised communal facilities for mentally retarded adults: I. Introduction. *American Journal of Mental Deficiency, 85*, 219-228.

Berkson, G., & Romer, D. (1980b). Social ecology of supervised communal facilities for mentally retarded adults: I. Introduction. *American Journal of Mental Deficiency, 85*, 219-228.

Berney, T. P., & Jones, P. M. (1988). Manic depressive disorder in mental handicap. *Australia and New Zealand Journal of Developmental Disabilities, 14*, 219-225.

Betz, N. E., Klien, K. L., & Taylor, K. M. (1996). Evaluation of a short form of career decision making self-efficiacy scale. *Journal of Career Assessment, 4*, 47-57.

Borthwick-Duffy, S. A. (1994). Epidemiology and prevalence of psychopathology in persons with mental retardation. *Journal of Consulting and Clinical Psychology, 62*, 17-27.

Bouras, N., & Brooks, D., Drummond, C. (1992). Community psychiatric services for people with mental retardation. In N. Bouras (Ed.), *Mental health in mental retardation*. New York: Cambridge University Press.

Bouras, N., & Drummond, C. (1992). Behavior and psychiatric disorders of people with mental handicaps living in the community. *Journal of Intellectual Disability Research, 36*, 349-357.

Bruininks, R. H., Hill, B. K., & Morreau, L. E. (1988). Prevalence and implications of maladaptive behaviors and dual diagnosis in residential and other service programs. In J. A. Stark, F. J. Menolascino, M. H. Albarelli, & V. C. Gray (Eds.), *Mental retardation and mental health: Classification, diagnosis, treatment, services* (pp. 3-29). New York: Springer-Verlag,.

Bruininks, R. H., Hill, B. K., Weatherman, R. F., & Woodcock, R. W. (1986). *Technical summary for the Inventory for Client and Agency Planning*. Allen, TX: DLM Teaching Resources.

Butcher, J. N., Dahlstrom, W.G., Graham, J.R., Tellegen, A., & Kaemmer, B. (1989). *MMPI-2:a Minnesota Multiphasic Personality Inventory-2*. Minneapolis: University of Minnesota.

Butterworth, J., Hagner, D., Hikkinen, B., De Mello, S., & McDonough, K. (1993). *Whole life planning: A guide for organizers and facilitators.* Boston: Children's Hospital, Institute for Community Inclusion.

Butterworth, J., Whitney-Thomas, J., & Steere, D. (1997). Using person-centered planning to address personal quality of life. In R. Schalock (Ed.). *Quality of life: Its application to persons with disabilities (Vol. II, pp. 5-23).* Washington, D.C.: American Association on Mental Retardation.

Cacioppo, J. T., Petty, R. E., Feinstein, J. A., Jarvis, W. B. (1996). Dispositional differences in cognitive motivation: The life and times of individuals varying in need for cognition. *Psychological Bulletin, 119,* 197-253.

Carr, E. G., & Durand, V. M. (1985a). The social-communicative basis of severe behavior problems in children. In S. Reiss & R. R. Bootzin (Eds.), *Theoretical issues in behavior therapy.* New York: Academic Press.

Carr, E. G., & Durand, V. M. (1985b). Reducing behavior problems through functional communication training. *Journal of Applied Behavior Analysis, 18,* 111-126.

Carver, C. S. (2000). On the continuous calibration of happiness. *American Journal on Mental Retardation, 105,* 336-341.

Charlot, L. R., Doucette, A., & Mezzacappa, E. (1993). Affective symptoms of institutionalized adults with mental retardation. *American Journal on Mental Retardation, 98,* 408-416.

Charlot, L., Deutsch, C., Hunt, A., Fletcher, K., & McIlvane, W. (2007). Validation of the mood and anxiety semi-structured (MASS) interview for patients with intellectual disabilities. *Journal of Intellectual Disability Research, 51,* 821-834.

Chiodo, J., & Maddux, J. E. (1985). A cognitive and behavioural approach to anxiety management of retarded individuals: Two case studies. *Journal of Child and Adolescent Psychotherapy, 2,* 16-29.

Clarke, D. J. (2001). Treatment of schizophrenia. In A. Dosen & K. Day (Eds.), *The treatment of mental illness and behavioral disorders in men-*

tally retarded children and adults. Washington, DC: American Psychiatric Association.

Cooper, S., Smiley, E., Morrison, J., Williamson, & Allan, L. (2007). Mental ill-health in adults with intellectual disabilities: Prevalence and associated factors. *British Journal of Psychiatry, 198,* 27-35.

Corbett, J. (1979). Psychiatric morbidity and mental retardation. In F. E. James & R. P. Snaith (eds.), *Psychiatric illness and mental handicap* (pp. 11-25). London: Gaskell.

Costa, P. T., & McCrae, R. (1992). *NEO-PI-R Professional Manual.* Odessa, Fl: Psychological Assessment Resources.

Craft, M. (1959). Mental disorder in the defective: A psychiatric survey of in-patients. *American Journal of Mental Deficiency, 63,* 329-334.

Crocker, A. C. (2000). Introduction: The happiness in all our lives. *American Journal on Mental Retardation, 105,* 319-325.

Crocker, A. G., Mercier, C., Allaire, J. F., & Roy, M.E. (2007). Profiles and correlates of aggressive behaviour among adults with intellectual disabilities. *Journal of Intellectual Disability Research, 51,* 786-801.

Crowne, D. P., & Marlowe, D. (1960). A new scale of social desirability independent of psychopathology. *Journal of Consulting Psychology, 24,* 349-354.

Crumbaugh, J.C., & Maholick, L.T. (1964). An experimental study in existentialism: The psychometric approach to Frankl's concept of noogenic neurosis. *Journal of Clinical Psychology, 20,* 200-2007.

Cullinan, D., Epstein, M. H., & Olinger, E. (1983). School behavior problems of mentally retarded and normal females. *The Mental Retardation and Learning Disability Bulletin, 11,* 104 109.

Cutts, R. A. (1957). Differentiation between pseudo-mental defectives with emotional disorders and mental defectives with emotional disturbances. *American Journal of Mental Deficiency, 61,* 761-772.

Davidson, M. (1988). Psychometric characteristics of the Checklist of Emotional Problems with Mentally Retarded Adults (CHEMRA). Unpublished doctoral dissertation, Department of Psychology, University of Illinois at Chicago.

Deci, E. L., Koestner, R., & Ryan, R. M. (1999). A meta-analytic review of experiments examining the effects of extrinsic rewards on intrinsic motivation. *Psychological Bulletin, 125,* 627-668.

Deci, E. L., & Ryan, R. M. (1985). *Intrinsic motivation and self-determination in human behavior.* New York: Plenum.

Deci, E. L. (1975). *Intrinsic motivation.* New York: Plenum.

De Waal, F. (1989). *Peacemaking among primates.* Cambridge, MA: Harvard University Press.

Dewan, J. G. (1948). Intelligence and emotional stability. *American Journal of Psychiatry, 104,* 548-554.

Dollard, J., Doob, L. W., Miller, N. E., Mowrer, O. H., & Sears, R. R. (1939). Frustration and aggression. New Haven, CT: Yale University.

Dosen, A., & Gielsen, J. (1993) Depression in the mentally retarded – Assessment and diagnosis. In R. Fletcher & A. Dosen (Eds.), *Mental health aspects of mental retardation: Progress in assessment and treatment.* New York: Lexington Books.

Duff, R., LaRocca, J.I., Lizzet, A., Martin, P., Pearce, L., Williams, M., & Peck, C. (1981). A comparison of the fears of mildly retarded adults with children of their mental age and chronological age matched controls. *Journal of Behavior Therapy and Experimental Psychiatry, 12,* 121-124.

Dumas, S., de la Garza, D., Seay, P., & Becker, H. (2002). "I don't know how they made it happen but they did": Efficacy perceptions in using a person centered approach. In S. Holburn & P. Vietze (Eds.), *Person centered planning: research, practice and future directions* (pp. 223 246). Baltimore, MD: Brookes.

Dunlap, K. (1919). Are there any instincts? *Journal of Abnormal Psychology, 14*, 307-311.

Dykens, E. M. (2006). Toward a positive psychology of mental retardation. *American Journal of Orthopsychiatry, 76*, 185-193.

Dykens, E. M., & Rosner, B. A. (1999). Refining behavioral phenotypes: Personality motivation in Williams and Prader-Willi syndromes. *American Journal of Mental Retardation, 104*, 158-169.

Eaton, L. F., & Menloascino, E. J. (1982). Psychiatric disorders in the mentally retarded: Types, problems, and challenges. *American Journal of Psychiatry, 139*, 1297-1303.

Eberstein, A. O. (1991). *The greatest happiness principle: An examination of utilitarianism.* New York: Garland.

Edgerton, R. R. (1967). *The cloak of competence: Stigma in the lives of the mentally retarded.* Berkeley: University of California Press.

Einfeld, S., & Wurth, P. (1989). Manic depressive disorder in mental handicaps. *Australia & New Zealand Journal of Developmental Disabilities, 15*, 155-156.

Eisenberger, R., & Cameron, J. (1996). The detrimental effects of reward: Myth or reality. *American Psychologist, 51*, 1153-1166.

Engel, G., Olson, K. R., & Patrick, C. (2002). The personality of love: Fundamental motives and traits related to components of love. *Personality and Individual Differences, 32*, 839-853.

Epstein, M. H., Cullinan, D., & Polloway, E. A. (1986). Patterns of maladjustment among mentally retarded children and youth. *American Journal of Mental Deficiency, 91*, 127-134.

Eron, L. D., & Huesmann, L. R. (1990). The stability of aggressive behavior – Even into the third generation. In M. Lewis and S. M. Miller (Eds.), *Handbook of developmental psychology* (pp. 147-156). New York: Plenum.

Esbensen, A. J., Rojahn, R., Aman, M. G., & Ruedrich, S. (2003). Reliability and validity of an assessment instrument for anxiety, depression, and mood among individuals with mental retardation. *Journal of Autism and Developmental Disorders, 33*, 617-629.

Eyman, R. K., & Borthwick, S. A. (1980). Patterns of care for mentally retarded persons. *Mental Retardation, 18*, 63-66.

Felce, D., & Perry, J. (1996). Exploring current conceptions of quality of life. In R. Renwick, I. Brown, & M. Nagler (Eds.). *Quality of life in health promotion and rehabilitation: Conceptual approach hes, issues, and applications*. Thousand Oaks, CA: Sage Publications.

Fletcher, R., Loschen, E., Stavrakaki, C., & First, M. (Eds.). (2007a). *Diagnostic manual – intellectual disability (DM-ID): A textbook of diagnosis of mental disorders in persons with intellectual disability.* Kingston, NY: NADD Press.

Fletcher, R., Loschen, E., Stavrakaki, C., & First, M. (Eds.). (2007b). *Diagnostic manual intellectual disability (DM-ID): A clinical guide for diagnosis of mental disorders in persons with intellectual disability.* Kingston, NY: NADD Press.

Fredrickson, B. L. (2001). The role of positive emotions in positive psychology: The broaden-and-build theory of positive emotions. *American Psychologist, 56*, 216-226.

Freeman, K. A., Anderson, C. M., Azer, R. H., Girolami, P. A., & Scotti, J. R. (1998). Why functional analysis is enough: A response to Reiss and Havercamp. *American Journal of Mental Retardation, 103*, 80-91.

Freud, S. (1963). *Introductory lectures on psychoanalysis*. London: Hogarth Press. (Original work published in 1916).

Gardner, W. I. (1967). Occurrence of severe depressive reactions in the mentally retarded. *American Journal of Psychiatry, 124*, 386-388.

Geschwind, D. H., & Dykens, E. (2004). Neurobehavioral and psychological issues in Klinefelter syndrome. *Learning Disabilities Research & Practice, 19* (3), 66-173.

Goldsmith, L., & Schloss, P. J. (1984). Diagnostic overshadowing among learning-disabled and hearing-impaired learners with an apparent secondary diagnosis of behavior disorders. *International Journal of Partial Hospitalization, 2,* 209-217.

Greenspan, S. B., & Granfield, J. M. (1992). Reconsidering the construct of mental retardation: Implications of a model of social competence. *American Journal of Mental Deficiency, 96*, 442-453.

Greenspan, S. B., & Shoultz, B. (1981). Why mentally retarded adults lose their jobs: Social competence as a factor in work adjustment. *Applied Research in Mental Retardation, 2*, 23-38.

Guarnaccia, V. J., & Weiss, R. L. (1974). The structure of fears in the mentally retarded. *Journal of Clinical Psychology, 30*, 540-545.

Guralnick, M. J. (1973). Behavior therapy with an acrophobic mentally retarded young adult. *Journal of Behavior Therapy and Experimental Psychiatry, 4*, 263-265.

Gustafsson, C., & Sonnander, K. (2002). Psychometric evaluation of a Swedish version of the Reiss Screen for Maladaptive Behavior. *Journal of Intellectual Disability Research, 46*, 218-229.

Hatton, C., & Emerson, E. (2004). The relationship between life events and psychopathology amongst children with intellectual disabilities. *Journal of Applied Research in Intellectual Disabilities, 17*, 109-177.

Havercamp, S.H. (1998). *The Reiss Profile of motivation sensitivity: Rreliability, validity, and social desirability.* Doctoral dissertation: Department of Psychology, Ohio State University.

Havercamp, S. H., & Reiss, S. (1997). The Reiss Screen for Maladaptive Behavior: Confirmatory factor analysis. *Behavior Research and Therapy, 35*, 967-971.

Havercamp, S. M., Reiss, S. (1996). Composite versus multiple rating scales in the assessment of psychopathology in people with mental retardation. *Journal of Intellectual Disabilities Research, 40*, 176-179

Havercamp, S.H., & Reiss, S. (2003). A comprehensive assessment of human striving: Reliability and validity of the Reiss Profile. *Journal of Personality Assessment, 81*, 123-132.

Heller, T. (1982). Social disruption and residential relocation of mentally retarded children. *American Journal of Mental Deficiency, 87*, 48-55.

Heller, T., Factor, A., Sterns, H., & Sutton (1996). Impact of person-centered later life planning training program for older adults with mental retardation. *American Journal of Mental Retardation, 62*, 77-83.

Herskovitz, H. H., & Plesset, M. R. (1941). Psychoses in adult mental defectives. *Psychiatric Quarterly, 15*, 574-588.

Hill, K. T. (1972). Anxiety in the evaluative context. In W. W. Hartup (ed.), *The young child: Review of research* (vol. 2, pp. 225-263). Washington, D.C.: National Association for the Education of Young Children.

Hjelle, L. A., & Bernard, M. (1994). Private self-consciousness and the retest reliability of self-reports. *Journal of Research in Personality, 28*, 52-67.

Holburn, S., & Vietze, P. (2002). *Person-centered planning: Research, practice, and future directions.* Baltimore: Paul H. Brookes.

Holburn, S., Gordon, A., & Vietze, P. M. (2007). *Person-centered planning made easy: The picture method.* Baltimore: Paul H. Brookes.

Huang, H., & Ruedrich, S. (2007). Recent advances in the diagnosis and treatment of attention deficit/hyperactivity disorder in individuals with intellectual disability. *Mental Health Aspects of Developmental Disabilities, 10*, 1-9.

Hull, C. L. (1943). *Principles of behavior.* New York: Appleton Century.

Hunt, J. M. (1971). Toward a history of intrinsic motivation. In H. I. Day, D. E. Berlyne., D. E. Hunt (Eds.), *Intrinsic motivation: A new direction in education.* Toronto: Holt, Rinehart and Winston.

Inwood, B., & Gerson, L.P. (1994). *The Epicurus reader.* Indianapolis, IN: Hackett Publishing co.

Irwin, T. (1995). *Plato's ethics*. New York: Oxford University Press.

Jackson, D. N. (1984). *Personality Research Form manual*. Port Huron, MI: Research Psychologists Press.

Jacobson, J. W. (1990). Do some mental disorders occur less frequently among persons with mental retardation? *American Journal on Mental Retardation, 94*, 596-602.

Jacobson, J. W. (1982a). Problem behavior and psychiatric impairment within a developmentally disabled population. I. Behavior frequency. *Applied Research in Mental Retardation, 3*, 121-139.

Jacobson, J. W. (1982b). Problem behavior and psychiatric impairment within a developmentally disabled population. II. Behavior severity. *Applied Research in Mental Retardation, 3*, 369-381.

James, D. H. (1986). Psychiatric and behavioural disorders amongst older mentally handicapped inpatients. *Journal of Mental Deficiency Research, 30*, 341-345.

James, W. (1918). *The principles of psychology* (vol. 2). New York: Dover. (Original work published in 1890).

Johns, M., & McDaniel, W. F. (1998). Areas of convergence and discordance between the MMPI-168 and the Reiss screen for maladaptive behavior in mentally retarded clients. *Journal of Clinical Psychology, 54*, 529-535.

Jopp, D. A., & Keys, C. B. (2001). Diagnostic overshadowing reviewed and reconsidered. *American Journal on Mental Retardation, 106*, 416-435.

Judah, S. M. (2006). *Staying together when an affair pulls you apart*. Downers Grove, IL: IVP Books.

Kavanaugh, P., & Reiss, S. (2001). *Why high school students get poor grades*. Unpublished manuscript. IDS Publishing.

Kessler, J. W. (1988). *Psychopathology of childhood (2nd ed.)*. Englewood Cliffs, NJ: Prentice -Hall.

King, N.J., Ollendick, T. H., Gullone, E., Cummins, R. A., & Josephs, A. (1990). Fears and phobias in children and adolescents with intellectual disabilities: Assessment and intervention strategies. *Australia and New Zealand Journal of Developmental Disabilities, 16*, 97-108.

Kishore, M. T., Nizamie, S. H, & Nizamie, A. (2005). The behavioural profile of psychiatric disorders in persons with intellectual disability. *Journal of Intellectual Disability Research, 49*, 852-857.

Kishore, M. T., Nizamie, A, Nizamie, S. H., & Jahan, M. (2004). Psychiatric diagnosis in persons with intellectual disability in India. *Journal of Intellectual Disability Research, 48*, 19-24.

Knapp, L. G., Barrett, R. P., Groden, G., & Groden, J. (1992). The nature and prevalence of fears in developmentally disabled children and adolescents: A preliminary investigation. *Journal of Development and Physical Disabilities, 4*, 195-203.

Knights, R. M. (1963). Test anxiety and defensiveness in institutionalized and non-instituionalized normal and retarded children. *Child Development, 34*, 1019-1026.

Kohn, A. (1993). *Punished by rewards*. Boston: Houghton Mifflin Company.

Koller, H., Richardson, S., Katz, M., & McLaren, J. (1983). Behavior disturbance since childhood among a 5-year birth cohort of all mentally retarded young adults in a city. *American Journal of Mental Deficiency, 87*, 386-395.

Kopp, C. B., Baker, B. L., & Brown, K. W. (1992). Social skills and their correlates: Preschoolers with developmental delays. *American Journal of Mental Deficiency, 96*, 357-366.

Kovacs, M. (1985). The children's depression inventory (CDI). *Psychopharmacology Bulletin, 21*, 995-998.

Krauss, M. W., Seltzer, M. M., & Goodman, S. J. (1992). Social support networks of adults with mental retardation who live at home. *American Journal of Mental Deficiency, 96*, 432-441.

Lakin, C., Doljanic, R., Taub, S., Giuseppina, C., & Byun, S. (2007). Adults with dual diagnoses of intellectual and psychiatric disability receiving Medicaid Home and Community-Based Services (HCBS) and ICF/ MR recipients in six states. *Mental Health Aspects of Developmental Disabilities, 10*, 78-91.

Lakin, C., Hill, B. K., Hauber, F. A., Bruininks, R. H., & Heal, L. W. (1983). New admissions and readmissions to a national sample of public residential facilities. *American Journal of Mental Deficiency, 88*, 13-20.

Laman, D. S. (1989). A longitudinal investigation of the relationship among depressed mood, social support, and social skills in mentally retarded adults. Unpublished doctoral dissertation, Department of Psychology, University of Illinois at Chicago.

Laman, D.L., & Reiss, S. (1989). The Illinois-Chicago mental health program. In R. Fletcher and F. Menolascino (eds.), *Mentally retarded and mentally ill: Assessment, treatment, and services for the dually diagnosed* (pp. 187-201). New York: D.C. Heath and Company.

Laman, D. S., & Reiss, S. (1987). Social skill deficiencies associated with depressed mood of mentally retarded adults. *American Journal of Mental Deficiency, 92*, 224-229.

Lancioni, G. E., Singh, N. N., O'Reilly, M. F., Oliva, D., & Basili, G. (2005). An overview of research on increasing indicies of happiness of people with severe/profound intellectual and multiple disabilities. *Disability and Rehabilitation, 27*, 83-93.

Larson, S. A., & Lakin, K. C. (1992). *Quality of life for people with challenging behavior living in community settings.* This study was presented at the 1992 annual AAMR national convention in New Orleans.

Lecavalier, L., & Havercamp, S. M. (2004). Are caregivers' reports of motivation valid? Reliability and validity of the Reiss profile MR/DD. *Journal of Intellectual Disability Research, 48*, 217-224.

Lecavalier, L., Tasse, M. J. (2005). An exploratory study of the "personality" of adolescents and adults with Down syndrome. *Journal of Intellectual and Developmental Disability, 30*, 67-74.

Lecavalier, L., & Tasse, M. J. (2003). Temporal stability and accuracy of motivational profile. *American Journal on Mental Retardation, 108,* 194-201.

Lecavalier, L., & Tasse, M. J. (2002). Sensitivity theory of motivation and psychopathology: An exploratory study. *American Journal on Mental Retardation, 107,* 105.115.

Lecavalier, L., & Tasse, M. J. (2001). Tranuction en adaption transculturelle du Reiss Screen for Maladaptive Behavior. *Revue Francophone de la deficience intellectuelle, 12,* 31-44.

Lepper, M.R. Corpus, J., & Lyengar, S. S. (2005). Intrinsic and extrinsic motivational orientations in the classroom: Age differences and academic correlates. *Journal of Educational Psychology, 97,* 184-196.

Lepper, M., Greene, D., & Nisbett, R. E. (1975). Undermining children's intrinsic interest with extrinsic reward: A test of the "overjustification" hypothesis. *Journal of Personality and Social Psychology, 28,* 129-137.

Levitan, G. W., & Reiss, S. (1983). Generality of diagnostic overshadowing across disciplines. *Applied Research in Mental Retardation, 4,* 59-69.

Linden, B. E., & Forness, S. R. (1986). Post-school adjustment of mentally retarded persons with psychiatric disorders: A ten-year follow-up. *Education and Training of the Mentally Retarded, 21,* 157-164.

Lindsay, W. R., & Michie, A. M. (1988). Adaptation of the Zung self-rating anxiety scale for people with a mental handicap. *Journal of Mental Deficiency Research, 32,* 485-490.

Luftig, R. L. (1988). Assessment of the perceived school loneliness and isolation of mentally retarded and nonretarded students. *American Journal on Mental Retardation, 92,* 472-475.

Lund, J. (1985). The prevalence of psychiatric morbidity in mentally retarded adults. *Acta Psychiatrica Scandinavia, 72,* 563-570.

Lunsky, Y. (2004). Suicidality in a clinical and community sample of adults with mental retardation. *Research in Developmental Disabilities, 25,* 231-243.

Lunsky, Y. (1999). *Sensitivity theory: How it relates to problem behavior and duality of life*. Paper presented at the annual meeting of the American Association on Mental Retardation, New Orleans.

Lunsky, Y., & Havercamp, S. M. (1999). Distinguishing low levels of social support and social strain: Implications for dual diagnosis. *American Journal on Mental Retardation, 104*, 200-204.

Lustman, N., & Zigler, E. (1982). Imitation by institutionalized and noninstitutionalized mentally retarded children and nonretarded children. *American Journal of Mental Deficiency, 87*, 252-258.

Lyubomirsky, S. (2007). *The how of happiness: A scientific approach to getting the life you want*. New York; Penguin.

Malcolm, N. (1966). Behaviorism as a philosophy. In T. Wann (Ed.), *Behaviorism and phenomenology*. Chicago: The University of Chicago Press.

Mandel, H. P. (1997). *Conduct disorder and underachievement: Risk factors, assessments, treatments, and prevention*. New York: Wiley.

Marsh, H. W., & Barnes, J. (1982). *Self-description questionnaire*. Unpublished manuscript, University of Sydney, Sydney, Australia.

Maslow, A. H. (1954). *Motivation and Personality*. New York: Harper & Row.

Mason, J., Scior, K. (2004). 'Diagnostic Overshadowing' amongst clinicians working with people with intellectual disabilities in the UK. *Journal of Applied Research in Intellectual Disabilities, 17*, 85-90.

Matson, J. L. (1982). Treating obsessive-compulsive behavior in mentally retarded adults. *Behavior Modification, 6*, 551-567.

Matson, J. L. (1981). Assessment and treatment of clinical fears in mentally retarded children. *Journal of Applied Behavior Analysis, 14*, 287-294.

Matson, J. L., Coe, D. A., Gardner, W. I., & Sovner, R. (1991). A factor analytic study of the diagnostic assessment fro the severely handicapped scale. *The Journal of Nervous and Mental Disease, 179*, 553-557.

Matson, J.L., Kazdin, A.E., & Senatore, V. (1984). Psychometric properties of the Psychopathology Instrument for Mentally Retarded Adults. *Applied Research in Mental Retardation, 4*, 399-407.

McClelland, D.C. (1967). *The achieving society*. Princeton, NJ: Van Nostrand.

McDougall, W. (2003). *An introduction to social psychology*. Mineola, NY: Dover (Originally published in 1908).

McNally, R. J. (2003). *Remembering trauma*. Cambridge, MA: Belknap Press/Harvard University Press.

McNally, R. J. (2002). Anxiety sensitivity and panic disorder. *Biological Psychiatry, 52*, 938-946.

McNally, R. J. (1991). Anxiety and phobias. In J. L. Matson & J. A. Mulick (Eds.), *Handbook of mental retardation* (pp. 413-423). New York: Pergamon.

McNally, R. J., & Ascher, L. M. (1987). Anxiety disorders in mentally retarded people. In L. Michelson & L. M. Ascher (Eds.), *Anxiety and stress disorders*. New York: Guilford.

McNally, R. J., & Calamari, J. E. (1988). Neuroleptic malignant syndrome in a man with mental retardation. *Mental Retardation, 26*, 385-386.

McNally, R. J., & Shin, L. M. (1994). Association of intelligence with severity of posttraumatic stress disorder symptoms in Vietnam combat disorder. *American Journal of Psychiatry, 152*, 936-938.

Meins, W. (1993). Prevalence and risk factors for depressive disorders in adults with intellectual disability. *Australia and New Zealand Journal of Developmental Disabilities, 18*, 147-156.

Menninger, K. (1938). *Man against himself*. New York: Harcourt, Brace, & World.

Menolascino, F. J. (1965). Emotional disturbance and mental retardation. *American Journal of Mental Deficiency, 70*, 248-256.

Menolascino, F. J., Lazer, J., & Stark, J. A. (1989). Diagnosis and management of depression and suicidal behavior in persons with severe mental retardation. *Journal of the Multihandicapped Person, 2,* 89-103.

Menolascino, F. J., & Stark, J. A. (1984). *Handbook of mental illness in the mentally retarded.* New York: Plenum.

Mill, J. S. (1873). *Autobiography.* New York: Holt.

Miller, N. E. (141). The frustration-aggression hypothesis. *Psychological Review, 48*, 337-342.

Miller, L. C., Barrett, C., Hampe, E., & Noble, H. (1971). Revised anxiety scales for the Louisville Behavioral Checklist. *Psychology Reports, 29*, 503-511.

Miller, M. L., Fee, V. E., & Jones, C. J. (2004). Psychometric properties of ADHD rating scales among children with mental retardation: II. Validity. *Research in Developmental Disabilities, 25*, 459-476.

Miller, M. L., Fee, V. E., Netterville, A. K. (2004). Psychometric properties of ADHD rating scales among children with mental retardation: I. Reliability. *Research in Developmental Disabilities, 25*, 459-476.

Monroe, M. J. (1987). Musical talent in mentally retarded individuals: A study of associated adaptive and maladaptive behavior. Unpublished masters thesis, Department of Psychology, University of Illinois at Chicago.

Mount. B., & Zwernik, K. (1988). *It's never too early, it's never too late: A booklet about personal futures planning.* St. Paul, MN: Metropolitan Council.

Mount, B. (1994). Benefits and limitations of personal futures planning. In V. J. Bradley, J. W. Ashbaugh, & Blaney, B. C. (1994), *Creating individual supports for people with developmental disabilities: A mandate for change at many levels.* Baltimore: P. H. Brookes.

Mundy, P. C., Seibert, J. M., & Hogan, A. E. (1985). Communication skills in the mentally retarded. In M. Sigman (Ed.), *Children with emotional disorders and developmental disabilities.* Orlando, Fl.: Grune & Stratton.

Murphy, G. (1929). *A historical introduction to modern psychology.* New York: Harcourt, Brace and Company.

Murray, H. A. (1943). Thematic Apperception Test. Cambridge, MA: Harvard University Press.

Murray, H. A. (1938). *Explorations in personality: A clinical and experimental study of fifty men of college age.* New York: Oxford University Press.

Myrbakk, E., Tetzchner, S. V. (2008). Screening individuals with intellectual disabilities for psychiatric disorders: Comparison of four measures. *American Journal of mental Retardation, 113,* 54-70.

Myers, I. B., McCaulley, M. H., Quenk, N. L., & Hammer, A. L. (1998). *Manual, a guide to the development and use of the Myers-Briggs Type Indicator* (3rd ed.). Palo Alto, CA: Consulting Psychological Press.

Nezu, C. M., Nezu, A. M., & Gill-Weiss, M. J. (1992). *Psychopathology in persons with mental retardation: Clinical guidelines for assessment and treatment.* Champaign, IL: Research Press.

Nihira, K., Leland, H., & Lambert, N. (1993). AMMR Adaptive Behavior Subscale – Residential and Community, 2nd edn. Pro-Ed, Austin, TX.

Novosel, S. (1984). Psychiatric disorder in adults admitted to a hospital for the mentally retarded. *British Journal of Mental Subnormality, 30,* 54-58.

Nucci, M., & Reiss, S. (1988). Mental retardation and emotional disturbance: A test for increased vulnerability to stress. *Australia and New Zealand Journal of Developmental Disabilities, 13,* 161-166.

Obler, M., & Terwilliger, R. E. (1970). Pilot study on the effectiveness of systematic desensitization with neurologically impaired children with phobic disorders. *Journal of Consulting and Clinical Psychiatry, 34,* 445-452.

O'Brien, J. (1987). A guide to lifestyle planning: Using the Activities Catalog to integrate services and natural supports systems. In B. Wilcox & G. T. Bellamy (Eds.), *The activities catalog: An alternative curriculum design for youth and adults with severe disabilities* (pp. 104-110). Baltimore: Paul H. Brookes.

O'Brien, C. L., & O'Brien, J. O. (2002). The origins of person-centered planning: A community of practice perspective. In S. Holburn & P. M. Vietze (Eds.), *Person-centered planning: Research, practice, and future directions*. Baltimore: Paul H. Brookes.

Ollendick, T. H. (1988). Reliability and validity of the revised Fear Survey Schedule for Children (FSSC-R*). Behaviour Research and Therapy, 21*, 685-692.

Olson, K.R. & Chapin, C. (2007). Relations of fundamental motives and psychological needs to well-being and intrinsic motivation. In Zelick, P. (Ed.), *Issues in the Psychology of Motivation*. Hauppauge, NY: Nova Science Publishers.

Olson, K. R., & Weber, D. (2004). Relations between big five traits and fundamental motives. *Psychological Reports, 95*, 795-802.

Park, L. (1998). Failure sensitivity, failure frequency, and test anxiety. Department of Psychology, Ohio State University. Library call number THE:PSY1998MAP374.

Philips, I. (1967). Psychopathology and mental retardation. *American Journal of Psychiatry, 124*, 67-73.

Philips, I., & Williams, N. (1975). Psychopathology and mental retardation: A study of 100 mentally retarded children. *American Journal of Psychiatry, 132*, 1265-1271.

Plato (1966). *The Republic of Plato*. New York: Oxford University Press. Translated by F. M. Cornford. Originally written in about 360 B.C.E.

Plehn, K., Peterson, R. A., & Williams, D. A. (1998). Anxiety sensitivity: Its relationship to functional status in patients with chronic pain. *Journal of Occupational Rehabilitation, 8*, 213- 222.

Prout, H. T. (1993). Assessing psychopathology in persons with mental retardation: A review of the Reiss Screen. *Journal of School Psychology, 31*, 535-540.

Rasmussen, S. A., & Tsuang, M. T. (1984). The epidemiology of obsessive-compulsive disorder. *Journal of Clinical Psychology, 45*, 450-457.

Reid, A. H. (1993). Schizophrenic and paranoid syndromes in persons with mental retardation: Assessment and diagnosis. In R. Fletcher & A. Dosen (Eds.), *Mental Health Aspects of Mental Retardation.* New York: Lexington Books.

Reid, A. H. (1980). Diagnosis of psychiatric disorders in the severely and profoundly retarded patient. *Journal of the Royal Society Medicine, 73,* 607-609.

Reid, A. H. (1976). Psychiatric disturbances in the mentally handicapped. *Proceedings of the Royal Society of Medicine, 69,* 509-512.

Reid, A. H. (1972a). Psychoses in adult mental defectives. I. Manic depressive psychosis. *British Journal of Psychiatry, 120,* 205-212.

Reid, A. H. (1972b). Psychoses in adult mental defectives. II. Schizophrenic and paranoid psychoses. *British Journal of Psychiatry, 120,* 213-218.

Reid, A.H., & Ballinger, B. R. (1987). Personality disorders in mental handicap. *Psychological Medicine, 17,* 983-987.

Reid, A.H., Ballinger, B. R., Heather, B. B., & Melvin, S. J. (1984). The natural history of behavioral symptoms among severely and profoundly mentally retarded patients. *British Journal of Psychiatry, 145,* 289-293.

Reid, A. H., & Naylor, G. J. (1976). Short cycle manic depressive psychosis in mental defectives: A clinical and physiological study. *Mental Deficiency Research, 20,* 67-76.

Reiss, S. (2009). Six motivational reasons for low school achievement. *Child and Youth Care Forum, 38,* 219-225.

Reiss, S. (2009). *Reiss Screen for Maladaptive Behavior test manual.* (2nd edition). Worthington, OH: IDS Publishing.

Reiss, S. (2008). *The normal personality: A new way of thinking about people.* New York: Cambridge University Press.

Reiss, S. (2005a). Extrinsic and intrinsic motivation at 30: Unresolved scientific issues. *Behavior Analyst, 28,* 1-14.

Reiss, S. (2004a). Multifaceted nature of intrinsic motivation: The theory of 16 basic desires. *Review of General Psychology, 8,* 179-193.

Reiss, S. (2004b). The 16 strivings for God. *Zygon, 39*, 303-320.

Reiss, S. (2000). *Who am I? The 16 basic desires that motivate our actions and define our personalities.* New York: Tarcher/Putnum.

Reiss, S. (1994). *Handbook of challenging behavior: Mental health aspects of mental retardation.* Worthington, OH: IDS Publishing Corporation.

Reiss, S. (1991). Expectancy model of fear, anxiety, and panic. *Clinical Psychology Review, 11*, 141-153.

Reiss, S. (1990a). Prevalence of dual diagnosis in community-based day programs in the Chicago metropolitan area. *American Journal of Mental Deficiency, 94*, 578-585.

Reiss, S. (1990). The development of a screening measure for psychopathology in people with mental retardation. In E. Dibble and D.B. Gray (eds.), *Assessment of behavior problems in persons with mental retardation living in the community* (pp. 107-118). Rockville, MD: National Institute of Mental Health.

Reiss, S. (1988). *The Reiss Screen for Maladaptive Behavior test manual.* Worthington, OH: IDS Publishing.

Reiss, S. (1985). The mentally retarded, emotionally disturbed adult. In M. Stigman (ed.), *Children with dual diagnosis: Mental retardation and mental illness* (pp. 171-192). New York: Grune & Stratton.

Reiss, S. (1982) Psychopathology and mental retardation: Survey of a developmental disabilities mental health program. *Mental Retardation, 20,* 128-132.

Reiss, S. (1980). Pavlovian conditioning and human fear: An expectancy model. *Behavior Therapy, 11*, 380-396.

Reiss, S., & Benson, B.A. (1985). Psychosocial correlates of depression in mentally retarded adults I: Minimal social support and stigmatization. *American Journal of Mental Deficiency, 89,* 331-339.

Reiss, S., & Benson, B.A. (1984). Awareness of negative social conditions among mentally retarded, emotionally disturbed outpatients. *American Journal of Psychiatry, 141*, 88-90.

Reiss, S., & Crouch, T. (2005). *Why people become organ donors?* Paper presented at the 133rd meeting of the American Public Health Association in Philadelphia.

Reiss, S., & Havercamp, S.M. (1998). Toward a comprehensive assessment of fundamental motivation. *Psychological Assessment, 10,* 97-106.

Reiss, S., Levitan, G.W., & McNally, R.J. (1982). Emotionally disturbed, mentally retarded people: An undeserved population. *American Psychologist, 37,* 361-367.

Reiss, S., Levitan, G.W., & Szyszko, J. (1982). Emotional disturbance and mental retardation: Diagnostic overshadowing. *American Journal of Mental Deficiency, 86,* 567-574.

Reiss, S., & McNally, R. J. (1985). Expectancy model of fear. In S. Reiss & R. R. Bootzin (Eds.), *Theoretical issues in behavior therapy.* New York, NY: Academic Press, pp. 107-121.

Reiss, S., Peterson, R.A., Gursky, D.M., & McNally, R.J. (1986). Anxiety sensitivity, anxiety frequency, and the prediction of fearfulness. *Behavior Research and Therapy, 24,* 1-8.

Reiss, S., Peterson, R.A., Taylor, S., Schmidt, N., & Weems, C. F. (2008). *Anxiety sensitivity index consolidated user manual: ASI, ASI-3, and CASI.* Worthington, OH: IDS Publishing Corporation.

Reiss, S. & Reiss, M. (2004) Curiosity and mental retardation: Beyond IQ. *Mental Retardation, 42,* 77-81.

Reiss, S., & Rojahn, J. (1993). Joint occurrence of depression and aggression in children and adults with mental retardation. *Journal of Intellectual Disability, 37,* 287-294.

Reiss, S., & Sushinsky, L.W. (1975). Overjustification, competing responses, and the acquisition of intrinsic interest. *Journal of Personality and Social Psychology, 31,* 1116-1125.

Reiss, S., & Szyszko, J. (1983). Diagnostic overshadowing and professional experience with mentally retarded persons. *American Journal of Mental Deficiency, 87,* 396-402.

Reiss, S., & Trenn, E. (1984). Consumer demand for outpatient mental health services for mentally retarded people. *Mental Retardation, 22*, 112-115.

Reiss, S., & Valenti-Hein, D. (1994). Development of a psychopathology rating scale for children with mental retardation. *Journal of Clinical and Consulting Psychology, 62*, 28-33.

Reiss, S., & Wiltz, J. (2008). Myers Briggs scales and psychological needs. Unpublished manuscript, Ohio State University.

Reiss, S. & Wiltz, J. (2004). Why people watch reality TV? *Media Psychology, 6*, 363-378.

Reiss, S., Wiltz, J., & Sherman, M. (2001). Trait motivational correlates of athleticism. *Journal of Personality and Individual Differences, 30,* 1139-1145.

Reynolds, W. M., & Baker, J. A. (1988). Assessment of depression in persons with mental retardation. *American Journal of Mental Retardation, 93*, 93-103.

Robertson, J., Hatton, C., Emerson, E., Elliott, J., McIntosh, B., Swift, P., et al. (2007). Reported barriers to the implementation of person-centered planning for people with intellectual disabilities in the UK. *Journal of Applied Research in Intellectual Disabilities, 20*, 297-307.

Robertson, J., Emerson, E., Hatton, C., Elliott, J., McIntosh, B., Swift, P., et al. (2006). Person-centered planning: Factors associated with successful outcomes for people with intellectual disabilities. *Journal of Intellectual Disability Research, 51*, 232-243.

Rojahn, J., Borthwick-Duffy, S. A., & Jacobson, J. W. (1993). The association between
psychiatric diagnoses and severe behavior problems in mental retardation. *Annals of Clinical Psychiatry, 5*, 163-170.

Romer, D., & Berkson, G. (1980). Social ecology of supervised communal facilities for mentally disabled adults: III. Predictors of social choice. *American Journal of Mental Deficiency, 85*, 243-252.

Rusch, F. R., DeStefano, L., Chadsey-Rusch, J., Phelps, I. A., & Szymanki, E. M. (1992). *Transition from school to adult life: Models, linkages, and policy.* Sycamore, IL: Sycamore Publishing.

Russell, A. T., & Tanguay, P. E. (1981). Mental illness and mental retardation: Cause or coincidence? *American Journal of Mental Deficiency, 85*, 570-574.

Rutter, M., Tizard, J., Yule, W., Graham, P., & Whitmore, K. (1976). Isle of Wight studies, 1964-1974. *Psychological Medicine, 6*, 313-332.

Ryan, R. (1994). Posttraumatic stress disorder in persons with developmental disabilities. *Community Mental Health Journal, 30*, 45-54.

Sacristan, J. R. (1987). Cross-cultural aspects on epidemiology in assessment of dual diagnosis. Featured paper presented at the International Research Conference on the Mental Health Aspects of Mental Retardation, Evanston, Illinois.

Schalock, R. L., & Harper, R. (1978). Placement from community-based mental retardation programs: How well do clients do? *American Journal of Mental Deficiency, 83,* 240-247.

Schalock, R. L., & Siperstein, G. N. (1996). *Quality of life.* Washington, D.C.: American Association on Mental Retardation.

Schloss, P. J. (1982). Verbal interaction patterns of depressed and nondepressed institutionalized mentally retarded adults. *Applied Research in Mental Retardation, 3*, 1-12.

Schmidt, N. B., & Cook, J. H. (1999). Effects of anxiety sensitivity on anxiety and pain during a cold pressor challenge in patients with panic disorder. *Behaviour Research and Therapy, 37*, 313-323.

Schmidt N.B., Lerew D.R., Jackson R.J. (1999). Prospective evaluation of anxiety sensitivity in the pathogenesis of panic: replication and extension. *Journal of Abnormal Psychology, 108*, 532–7.

Schmidt N.B., Lerew D.R., Jackson R.J. (1997). The role of anxiety sensitivity in the pathogenesis of panic: prospective evaluation of spontaneous panic attacks during acute stress. *Journal of Abnormal Psychology, 106*, 355–64.

Schmid, N.B., Zvolensky, M. J., Maner, J. K. (2006). Anxiety sensitivity: Prospective prediction of panic attacks and Axis I pathology. *Journal of Psychiatric Research, 40*, 691-699.

Silverman, W. K., Flesig, W., Rabian, B., & Peterson, R. A. (1991). Childhood Anxiety Sensitivity Index. *Journal of Clinical Child Psychology, 20*, 162-168.

Skinner, B. F. (1938). *The behavior of organisms: An experimental analysis.* New York: Appleton-Century-Crofts.

Smull, M. W., & Harrison (1992). *Supporting people with severe reputations in the community.* Alexandria, VA: National Association of State Mental Retardation Directors.

Sovner, R. (1986). Limiting factors in the use of DSM III criteria with mentally ill/ mentally retarded persons. *Psychopharmacology Bulletin, 22*, 1055-1059.

Sovner, R., & Hurley, A. D. (1983). Do the mentally retarded suffer from affective illness? *Archives of General Psychiatry, 40*, 61-67.

Sprengler, P. M., Strohmer, D. C., & Prout, H. T. (1990). Testing the robustness of diagnostic overshadowing bias. *American Journal on Mental Retardation, 95*, 204-273.

Stein, M.B., Jang, K. L., & Livesley, W. J. (1999). Heritability of anxiety sensitivity: A twin study. *American Journal of Psychiatry, 156*, 246-251.

Stein, M.B., Schork, N.J., & Gelenter, J. (2007). Gene-by-environment (serotonin transporter and childhood emotional maltreatment) interaction for anxiety sensitivity, an intermediate phenotype for depression and anxiety. *Neuropsychopharmacology, 33*, 312-319.

Stephens, E. (1953). Defensive reactions of mentally retarded adults. *Social Casework, 34*, 119-124.

Sternberg, R. J. (1998). *Cupid's arrow: The course of love through time.* London: Cambridge University Press.

Sternlicht, M., Pustel, G., & Deutsch, M. R. (1970). Suicidal tendencies among institutionalized retardates. *Journal of Mental Subnormality, 16,* 93-102.

Sturmey, P., & Bertman, L. J. (1994). Validity of the Reiss Screen for Maladaptive Behavior. *American Journal of Mental Retardation, 99,* 201-206.

Sugg, D. K. (1999, December 3). When am I going to go home? *The Baltimore Sun.* pp. A1, A8.

Suomi, S. J., Eiselle, C. D., Grady, S. A., & Harlow, H. F. (1975). Depressive behavior in adult monkeys following separation from family environment. *Journal of Abnormal Psychology, 84,* 576-578.

Switzky, H. N. (1999). Intrinsic motivation and motivational self systems. In E. Zigler, D. Bennet-Givens (Eds.), *Personality development in individuals with mental retardation.* New York: Cambridge University Press.

Szymanski, L. S. (2000). Happiness as a treatment goal. *American Journal on Mental Retardation, 105,* 352-362.

Szymanski, L. S. (1980). Psychiatric diagnosis in retarded persons. In L. S. Szymanski & P. E. Tanguay, (Eds.), *Emotional disorders of mentally retarded persons: Assessment, treatment, and consultation* (pp. 131-148). Baltimore: University Park Press,.

Szymanski, L. S., & Biederman, J. (1984). Depression and anorexia nervosa of persons with down syndrome. *American Journal of Mental Deficiency, 89,* 246-251.

Szymanski, L. S., & Tanguay, P. E. (1980). *Emotional disorders of mentally retarded persons.* Baltimore: University Park Press.

Tasse, M. J., Sabourin, G., Perreault, P., Labbe, L., Corbeil, L. Hill, A., et al. (2002). Le profil Reiss des buts foundamentaux et des sensibilities motivationnellas pour personnes presentant une deficience intellectuelle. Montreal: Department of Psychology, Universite du Quebec a Montreal.

Taylor, S. (Ed.), (1999). *Anxiety sensitivity: Theory, research, and treatment of the fear of anxiety*. Mahwah, NJ: Lawrence Erlbaum.

Taylor, S., Jang, K. L., Stewart, S. H., & Stein, M. B. (2008). Etiology of the dimensions of anxiety sensitivity: A behavioral-genetic analysis. *Journal of Anxiety Disorders, 22*, 899-914.

Tonge, B., & Einfeld, S. (2000). The trajectory of psychiatric disorders in young people with intellectual disabilities. *Australian and New Zealand Journal of Psychiatry, 34*, 80-84.

Thorndike, E. L. (1913). *Educational psychology (vol 1)*. New York: Columbia University.

Valenti-Hein, D. C., & Mueser, K. T. (1990). *The dating skills program: Reaching social-skills to adults with mental retardation*. Worthington, OH: IDS Publishing.

Van Minnen, A., Savelsberg, P. M., & Hoogduin, K. A. L. (1995). A Dutch version of the Reiss Screen for Maladaptive Behavior. *Research in Developmental Disabilities, 16*, 43-50.

Vitiello, B., Spreat, S., & Behard, D. (1989). Obsessive-compulsive disorder in mentally retarded patients. *Journal of Nervous and Mental Disease, 177*, 233-235.

Walsh, K. K., & Shenouda, N. (1999). Correlations among the Reiss Screen, the Adaptive Behavior Scale Part II, and the Aberrant Behavior Checklist. *American Journal on Mental Retardation, 104(3)*, 236-248.

Weems, C. F., Hayward, C., Killen, J. D., & Taylor, C. B. (2002). A longitudinal investigation of anxiety sensitivity in adolescence. *Journal of Abnormal Psychology, 111*, 471-477.

Wehmeyer, M. L., Kelchner, K., & Richards, S. (1996). Essential characteristics of self- determined behavior of individuals with mental retardation. *American Journal on Mental Retardation, 100*, 632-642.

Weiner, B. (1995). Intrinsic motivation. In A. Manstead, M. Hewstone, S. Fiske, M. Hoggs, H. Reis, & Samin, E (Eds.), *The Blackwell Encyclopedia of Social Psychology*. Cambridge: Blackwell.

White, R. W. (1959). Motivation reconsidered: The concept of competence. *Psychological Review*, 66, 297-333.

Widaman, E. J., MacMillan, K. F., Hemsley, D. L., Little, R. E., & Balow, I. H. (1992). Differences in adolescents' self-concept as a function of academic level, ethnicity, and gender. *American Journal on Mental Retardation. 96*, 387-403.

Williams, G. A., & Asher, S. R. (1992). Assessment of loneliness at school among children with mental retardation. *American Journal of Mental Retardation, 96*, 357-366.

Wiltz, J., & Reiss, S. (2003). Compatibility of housemates with mental retardation. *American Journal of Mental Retardation, 108*, 173-180.

Wiltz, J., Kalnins, T. (2008). Aggression, sociability, and roommate friendship: New findings translated into a resource for self-determined choices. *Journal of Policy and Practice in Intellectual Disabilities, 5*, 159-166.

Woodworth, R. S. (1928). How emotions are identified and classified. In M. L. Reymert (eds.), *How emotions are identified and classified.* Worcester, MA: Clark University.

Woodworth, R. S. (1918). *Dynamic psychology.* New York: Columbia University Press.

Zetlin, A. G., & Turner, J. L. (1984). Self-perspectives on being handicapped: Stigma and adjustment. In R. Edgerton (Ed.), *Lives in progress: Mentally retarded adults in a large city. AAMD Monographs, 6,* 93-120.

Zilboorg, G., & Henry, G. (1941). *A history of medical psychology.* New York: W. W. Norton.

Zigler, E. (1971). The retarded child as a whole person. In H. E. Adams & W. K. Boardman (Eds.), *Advances in experimental clinical psychology* (pp. 47-121). New York: Pergamon Press.

Zigler, E., & Bennet-Givens, D. (1999), *Personality development in individuals with mental retardation.* New York: Cambridge University Press.

Zigler, E., Bennet-Givens, D., & Hodapp, R. (1999). Assessing personality traits of individuals with mental retardation. In E. Zigler, D. Bennet-Givens (Eds.), *Personality development in individuals with mental retardation*. New York: Cambridge University Press.

Zung, W. (1971). A rating instrument for anxiety disorders. *Psychometrics, 12,* 371-379.

Subject Index